TONY PERROTTET is the author of *Pagan Holiday: On the Trail of Ancient Roman Tourists.* He has worked as a foreign correspondent in South America, a film extra in Rajasthan, and a freelance writer in New York, contributing to publications including *Esquire, Outside, The New York Times, Smithsonian, Condé Nast Traveler,* and *National Geographic Adventure.* He is Australian and lives in Manhattan with his wife and son.

THE NAKED
OLYMPICS

RANDOM HOUSE TRADE PAPERBACKS

NEW YORK

THE NAKED
OLYMPICS

THE TRUE STORY
OF THE ANCIENT GAMES

ILLUSTRATIONS BY LESLEY THELANDER

TONY PERROTTET

2004 Random House Trade Paperback Original

Text copyright © 2004 by Tony Perrottet

Film stills from *Olympia, Ben-Hur,* and *The 300 Spartans* are reproduced courtesy of Photofest.

Photographs on pages 4, 5, and 66 copyright © 2004 by Tony Perrottet

Illustrations are by Lesley Thelander and are reproduced courtesy of the illustrator.

Library of Congress Cataloging-in-Publication Data
Perrottet, Tony.
The naked Olympics: the true story of the ancient games / Tony Perrottet.
p.   cm.
ISBN 0-8129-6991-x
1. Olympic games (Ancient)   I. Title.
GV23.P47 2004   796.48—dc22   2003066728

Random House website address: www.atrandom.com

Printed in the United States of America

6 8 9 7 5

Book design by Victoria Wong

For Yvonne and John,
who inspired a love of
travel and history

If the Olympic Games were being held right now, you would see why we Greeks attach such paramount importance to athletics. Oh, I can't describe the scene in mere words. You really should experience firsthand the incredible pleasure of standing in that cheering crowd, admiring the athletes' courage and good looks, their amazing physical conditioning—their great skill and irresistible strength—all their bravery and their pride, their unbeatable determination, their unstoppable passion for victory!

I know that if you were there in the Stadium, you wouldn't be able to stop applauding.

—LUCIAN, *Anacharsis*, C. A.D. 140

Acknowledgments

THE STUDY OF the ancient Olympics is a crowded field, and one that I entered with some hesitation. Ever since the Victorian era, when modern interest in athletics was revived, scholars have pored over every detail of Greek physical culture. (Energetic dons at British universities even took to the arenas with handmade discuses and practiced running naked to see if it improved speed.) The volume of scholarship has only increased with the popularity of the modern Olympics, reborn in 1896 in Athens. Was it possible to say something fresh about a subject that invites a new spate of books every fourth year?

But reading through the voluminous literature, I realized that most serious works on the Olympics maintained a very narrow (and often excruciatingly dry) focus. Nobody had tried to recreate the ancient Games in their sprawling, human entirety—as the ultimate pagan festival, a mass gathering where the Greeks' favorite sports were combined with religious ceremonies and every possible ancient entertainment. To answer my own central question—What was the actual experience of attending this extravaganza?—I would need to write a different book. So I decided to approach the Games day by day, step by step, weaving together the strands of evidence to recapture what it was like to be a part of the ancient Olympics as a spectator, an athlete, or one of the overworked officials.

Naturally, this excursion into antiquity could not have been written without the help of many people.

I would particularly like to thank Dr. David Gilman Romano, senior researcher at the Mediterranean section of the University of Pennsylvania, for generously providing his time and advice. As both a classicist and a former track champion, he is uniquely qualified to connect ancient evidence with actual practice, and bring Greek sports to life. Of the many fine scholars working in the field, I must acknowledge a debt above all to James Davidson and Lionel Casson for their groundbreaking works on daily life in the ancient era, and to Stanley Lombardo for his luminous translation of Homer.

In Greece, while I was researching at ancient Olympia itself, Dr. Helmut Kyrieleis of the German Archaeological Institute very kindly showed me around the recent excavations and helped interpret many puzzling aspects of the site, while the experts Frank and Patricia, raising a column of the Temple of Zeus, kindly invited me to their home for dinner, providing the only square meal I had in modern Olympia, one of Greece's more mercenary service towns.

I would also like to offer my thanks to my excellent editor, Susanna Porter, for her ongoing encouragement and perceptive advice on the manuscript; her assistant, Evelyn O'Hara, who brought the strands of text and artwork seamlessly together; the inspired art director Robbin Schiff; my energetic agent, Elizabeth Sheinkman; and Rob Weissman, for his enthusiastic support and advice on modern athletics.

Of course, my broadest debt is to my wife, Lesley Thelander, who helped nurse this book from its earliest drafts; without her patient assistance, detailed editing, and regular infusions of humor, it would have remained a formless mass. Thanks finally to budding pentathlete Henry Perrottet, who kept me suitably fit while writing about ancient sports by running me ragged around the playgrounds of Manhattan and beaches of Sydney.

Contents

List of Illustrations

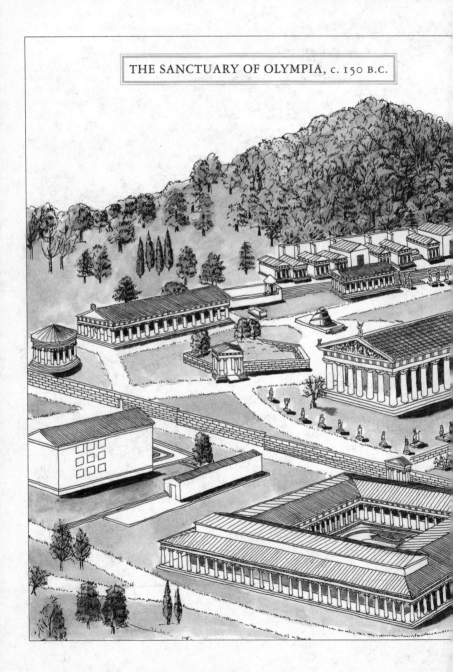

THE SANCTUARY OF OLYMPIA, c. 150 B.C.

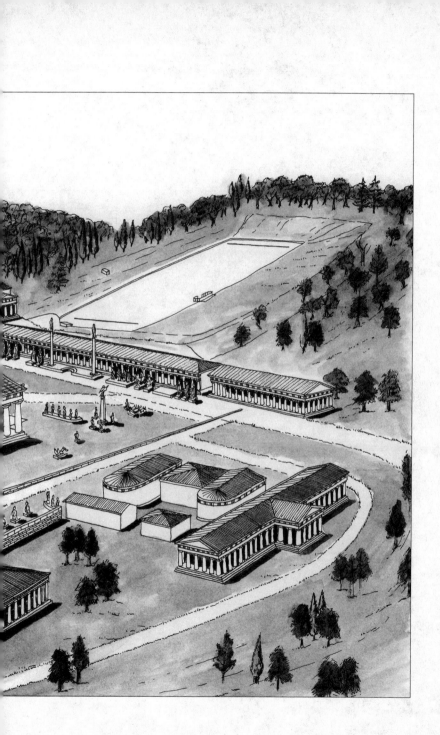

THE NAKED
OLYMPICS

I.

For the Love of Zeus

*(Greek) light acquires a transcendent quality: it is not the light
of the Mediterranean alone, it is something more, something un-
fathomable, something holy. Here the light penetrates directly to
the soul, opens the doors and windows of the heart, makes one
naked, exposed, isolated. . . . No analysis can go on in this light;
here the neurotic is either instantly healed or goes mad.*
 —HENRY MILLER, *The Colossus of Maroussi*

IN THE HILLS above Olympia, I awoke with a start before
dawn, feeling bleary-eyed from the Greek wine I'd drunk with
some rowdy archaeologists the night before. It was going to be a
perfect summer's day: From my hotel window I saw clear sky
over the mountains of Arcadia, whose peaks covered the horizon
like the waves of a wild blue sea. I needed some exercise—a jog
to clear my head. But where should I run in this corner of the
rural Peloponnese? Where else, it occurred to me, but in the ancient Olympic Stadium?

I arrived at the ruins just before the sun, wearing an old pair
of Nikes (named after the winged goddess of Victory). Even the
guards were only half awake, nursing their potent coffees beneath the olive trees, but they waved me through the gates, let-

Remains of the Stadium entrance for athletes, ancient Olympia.

ting me have the ultimate sports venue to myself. No tour buses would arrive for at least an hour to disturb my private Greek sanctuary. I followed a trail past the fallen columns of great temples, splayed out in the grass like skeletal fingers; purple wildflowers pushed up between memorials to forgotten sporting champions. Olympia's idyllic pastoral setting has changed little in the last twenty-five hundred years: the river Alpheus still gurgles in its shady bed alongside the Gymnasium; to the north rises an evenly conical hill, bristling with pine forest, where Zeus had wrestled his father, the Titan Kronos, for control of the world.

Soon a stone archway announced the entrance to the Stadium. My morning jog was suddenly starting to take on the contours of a redemptive ritual. The natural arena was bathed in golden light—that unmistakable Greek brilliance about which Henry Miller had rhapsodized, just as Lord Byron had a century earlier and the orator Cicero two millennia before that—the light that seems to pierce the centuries, molding the past with the present, blurring history with myth. Rising on each side of me were earth embankments, now swathed in succulent green lawn. And there, at the very center of the Stadium, was the running track—a rectangular expanse of clay, bordered by stone gutters, vaguely suggesting a small landing strip. According to archaic legend, the track's 210-yard length was originally marked out by the demigod Hercules himself. For nearly twelve centuries, it was the focus of the greatest recurring festival in Western history.

I approached the ancient starting line—a white marble sill that is miraculously intact—kicked off the Nikes, and instead curled my toes into the premade grooves. Nothing broke the silence except the buzzing of bees in the distance. And then I was off, racing in the footsteps of ancient champions—Greeks with magical names like Skamandros of Mytilene and Leonidas of Rhodes. During my weeks of reading about the original

The starting line at the eastern end of Olympia's Stadium. Runners placed their toes in the sill's grooves, and started from an upright position.

Olympic Games, these figures had always seemed unreal, illusory. But now, as my feet pounded the hard earth, it was easy to imagine a time when the gaze of ancient spectators and their gods was fixed on this spot—and on mere mortals like myself.

AROUND 150 B.C., as the first rays of dawn struck the Stadium, there would have been at least forty thousand spectators crowded onto those same green embankments, jostling cheek by jowl on the roughened turf. These were the die-hard sports fans of the ancient Greek world, and they came from every level of society, so that coiffed young aristocrats rubbed shoulders with callused fishermen, mathematicians with illiterate bakers. The majority of spectators were male—married women were forbidden to attend, although unmarried women and girls were allowed in the stands. But whether male or female, young or old, rich or poor, every eye was impatiently fixed on the straight running track, whose putty-colored clay had been covered by a layer of gleaming white sand.

Ten bearded judges in indigo robes and garlands of flowers would have taken their place in a booth halfway down the track, looking less like sporting officials than Indian wedding guests. Before them, on a table of ivory and gold, were the first Olympic medals—olive-wreath crowns cut from Olympia's sacred tree. And an excited murmur filled the Stadium when, with the blast of a trumpet, the athletes began to emerge from a tunnel built into the western hillside.

They appeared one by one—parading like peacocks, entirely unclothed and unadorned, yet dripping from head to toe in perfumed oils that flowed in rivulets from their curled black hair. Competing nude was a time-honored tradition of ancient Greek athletics, as much a part of Hellenic culture as drinking wine, discussing Homer, or worshiping Apollo; only barbarians were ashamed to display their bodies. Related to initiation rites, the practice also symbolically stripped away social rank, an extraordinary gesture toward a democratic sporting ideal in the status-obsessed ancient world (although contestants still had to be free-born males of Greek descent—women, slaves, and foreigners were beyond the pale). A sacred herald declared the name of each athlete, his father's name, and his home city before asking if any-one in the crowd had any charge to lay against him. After being announced, the contestants, to the cheers of admirers, warmed up with their trainers in the sun—a time-honored routine of running on the spot, practicing their starts and abruptly halting, dropping on their haunches, and stretching their hamstrings.

The cries and jeers of the crowd subsided when the sacred her-alds raised their trumpets, giving the call for the twenty athletes to "take their positions, foot to foot, at the *balbis*"—the marble starting line, with carved grooves for the runners' toes. Rather than a crouch, the traditional ancient starting position for sprinters was standing upright—leaning slightly forward, feet together, arms outstretched, every muscle poised. A rope was stretched before them at chest height, creating a rudimentary starting gate. Contestants eyed the barrier respectfully: the pun-ishment for false starts was a thrashing from the official whip bearers.

The chief judge nodded, the herald cried *ápete*—go!

And as the athletes sprinted down the track, the roar of the spectators exploded through the morning like a thunderclap, startling the sheep in the surrounding countryside.

FOR THOSE IN the crowd, it was a thrilling moment—a high point, Greek philosophers argued, of any citizen's life—if only they could forget their intense physical discomfort.

Surviving a day in the Stadium was worthy of an olive wreath in itself. The summer heat was oppressive even in the early morning, and many in the crowd would have been feeling the ef-fects of the previous night's revelries. It's just as well entry to the Olympics was free: For the next sixteen hours, spectators would be on their feet (the root meaning of the ancient Greek word *sta-dion* is actually "a place to stand"), their bare heads exposed to the endless sun and dramatic thunderstorms, while itinerant vendors extorted them for suspicious sausages, rock-hard bread, and dubious cheese, to be washed down with throat-scalding resinated wine. Most excruciating, there was no reliable water supply at Olympia—summer had reduced the local rivers to a trickle—so dehydrated spectators would be collapsing in droves from heatstroke. Nobody bathed for days. The sharp odor of sweat did battle with Olympia's fragrant pine forests and wild-flowers, only to be overpowered by the intermittent wafts from the dry riverbeds, which had been turned into open-air latrines. And every minute of the day was a trial with Olympia's incessant plagues of flies. The whole experience was so famously uncom-fortable that a master once threatened his disobedient slave with a visit to the Olympic Games.

Zeus, the king of the gods, would be admiring the festival from his celestial seat—he was known to follow the sports results as keenly as mortals—but the fans in the Stadium had been suf-fering indignities for weeks. The sanctuary of Olympia was lovely but remote, nestled in the southwest of Greece 210 miles southwest from Athens, so most spectators had traipsed rough mountain highways to attend; international visitors had risked storms and shipwreck to sail from as far away as Spain and the Black Sea.* When the exhausted crowds arrived, they found a venue sadly unprepared to host them. ". . . An endless mass of people," complained the second-century author Lucian, utterly swamped Olympia's modest facilities, creating conditions remi-niscent of a badly planned rock concert.

---

*There is a common confusion about the name of Olympia. The Greek gods lived on Mount Olympus—a rugged peak in Thessaly, in northern Greece. The sanctu-ary of Olympia, where the Games were held, lies in *southern* Greece, in the claw-shaped peninsula known as the Peloponnesus. Olympia's name echoes the mountain's, to emphasize its sanctity.

The only inn at ancient Olympia, the Leonidaion, was reserved for ambassadors and officials, so everyone else was left to fend for themselves. The Sacred Precinct of Zeus—a walled-off enclave of pagan temples and shrines—was besieged on all sides by a vast, anarchic campground, and the rowdy throngs all set to claiming their own space, in keeping with their station: Most simply flung their bedding wherever they could, huddling between altars, crowding elegant colonnades, nestling between the statues of illustrious sporting champions. Others rented space in temporary shelters or put up their own tents, sprawling like refugees across the surrounding countryside. Plato himself once slept in a makeshift barracks, head to toe with snoring, drunken strangers.

The smoke from thousands of cooking fires created a pall of pollution. Crowd control was enforced by local officials with whips.

Not for nothing does our word *chaos* derive from the ancient Greek; with its lack of basic sanitation or facilities, the Olympic festival was the Woodstock of antiquity.

For the five days of the Games—an action-packed program of athletics, chariot racing, boxing, and wrestling—conditions for spectators would continue to deteriorate. Rotting garbage was dropped into makeshift wells, including the bones of hundreds of sacrificial animals. The unhygienic conditions ensured that fevers and diarrhea began to rip through the crowd, a situation not helped by the maddening insect plagues: Before every Games, priests at Olympia sacrificed at an altar to "Zeus the Averter of Flies" in the forlorn hope of reducing the infestations. Even at the close of the festival, spectators could expect no relief: They could be stranded for days bargaining with wagon drivers for a ride home.

And yet, as the attendance figures suggest, none of these miseries could keep ancient sports fans away. The Games were sensationally popular, the greatest recurring event in antiquity, held without fail every four years from 776 B.C. until the Christian

Pentathletes enter the field, carrying (from left to right) *hand weights for the long jump, javelin, and discus. (From an Athenian amphora, a prize at the Panathenaic games, c. 525 B.C.)*

emperors banned pagan festivals in A.D. 394—a mind-boggling run of nearly twelve hundred years. For the Greeks, it was considered a great misfortune to die without having been to Olympia. One Athenian baker boasted on his gravestone that he had attended the Games twelve times. "By heaven!" raved the holy man Apollonius of Tyana. "Nothing in the world of men is so agreeable or dear to the Gods."

WHAT WAS THE secret of the Games' longevity? What kept the hordes coming back, generation after generation? It was a question that the Athenian philosopher and avid sports buff

Epictetus pondered late in the first century. He argued that the Olympics were a metaphor for human existence itself. Every day was filled with difficulties and tribulations: unbearable heat, pushy crowds, grime, noise, and endless petty annoyances. "But of course you put up with it all," he said, "because it's an unforgettable spectacle."

The Games of Life

TO RECAPTURE THE allure of the ancient Olympics, we have to realize that sports were only one part of the festival. The Games were actually the ultimate pagan entertainment package, where every human diversion could be found at once, on and off the field. Each Olympiad was an expression of Hellenic unity, an all-consuming pageant, the meeting place of heaven and earth, as spiritually profound for pagans as a pilgrimage to Varanasi for Hindus or the Muslim hajj. The site had grand procession routes, dozens of altars, public banquet halls, booths for sideshow artists. In terms of audience satisfaction, our own revived Olympic Games can hardly compare—unless they were to be combined with Carnival in Rio, Easter Mass at the Vatican, and a tour of Universal Studios.

For five hectic days and nights, Olympia was the undisputed capital of the world, and visitors hardly knew where to turn first. Splendid religious rituals were observed; in fact, the ceremonies, including the butchering of one hundred oxen for a grand public feast, took up as much time as the sports. There was sacred sightseeing to be done: the sanctuary of Olympia was an open-air museum, and visitors rushed between events from temple to temple, to view famous masterpieces like the forty-foot-high statue of Zeus, one of the seven wonders of the ancient world, which was proudly presented by volunteer tour guides, called *exegetai*. (These local experts were notoriously pushy and verbose. One pilgrim fervently prayed: "Zeus, protect me from your guides at Olympia!")

And then there were earthly pursuits: The squalid tent-city was the scene of a round-the-clock bacchanal where students would squander their inheritances in lavish *symposia* (drinking parties) and prostitutes could make a year's wages in five days. There were beauty contests, Homer-reading competitions, eating races. Expert masseurs offered rubdowns to the weary. Young boys in makeup performed erotic dances. Competing for attention were palm readers and astrologers, soap-box orators and fire-eaters, even, according to one observer, Dio the Golden-Tongued, "countless lawyers perverting justice" (orators discussing their upcoming prosecutions). Famous Greek writers presented new work on the temple steps. Actors declaimed, poets recited epic odes, painters shamelessly displayed their oeuvres and schmoozed with potential patrons. In fact, so much was going on that a starry-eyed pilgrim might be excused for forgetting about the athletic contests—if they weren't themselves so superbly theatrical.

No amount of pomp was spared on the field, with the colorful parades of athletes, trumpet-blowing heralds, and the recitation of dramatic oaths in front of menacing statues (in this era before steroids, judges were concerned that contestants might enhance their performance with magic). Of the eighteen core events in the Olympics program, some are familiar to us today—running, wrestling, boxing, javelin, discus. Others seem more outlandish. The Games began with the chariot race—a deliriously violent affair, where up to forty vehicles crowded the track and crashes were guaranteed. At times, only a handful or even a single chariot would complete the course. There was the *hoplitodromia,* a sprint in full armor. The long jump was performed with weights, to the accompaniment of flute music. And one of the favorite audience events was the *pankration*—a savage all-out brawl, where only eye gouging was banned. The more brutish participants would snap opponents' fingers, or tear out their intestines; the judges (one coach noted) "approve of strangling." The gaps in the program seem just as odd to modern eyes—there were no team sports, no ball sports, no swimming events, no marathon, and nothing resembling an Olympic torch—but nobody complained about a lack of entertainment on the field. Even the most thuggish of ancient strongmen were crowd-pleasing hams, playing up to audiences like World Wrestling Federation contestants today. Off the field, some dressed up like Hercules, wearing lion skins and carrying clubs; others would entertain their admirers by tossing enormous weights, or indulging in prodigious feats of gluttony.

In this heady, macho atmosphere, there was no shortage of scandals to gossip about: All the vices of our modern Games were present at their birth. Despite the Sacred Olympic Truce, which supposedly banned all wars that might interrupt the successful staging of the event, the ancient Games were often caught up in Greek internal politics: A military force once even attacked Olympia itself, in the middle of a wrestling match, forcing defenders into positions on top of the temples.

Corruption charges would regularly disgrace contenders. The first prosecution at Olympia occurred in 388 B.C., when a certain Eupolus of Thessaly bribed three boxers to throw their fights against him. Thereafter, cheats were heavily fined, and the cash used to erect statues with moral inscriptions reminding athletes that "you win at Olympia with the speed of your feet and the strength of your body, not with money." Even the judges were not above suspicion. In A.D. 67, they accepted hefty bribes from the Roman emperor Nero, agreeing to add poetry reading to the roster of contests and magnanimously awarding him first prize in the chariot race—despite the fact that he fell out of his vehicle and failed to complete the course.

In fact, money permeated every aspect of ancient athletics. The contestants were all professionals: They lived on stipends from civic bodies and private patrons, and traveled in troupes from one sporting event to the next, picking up lucrative cash prizes as they went. (Tellingly, the ancient Greeks did not even have a word for amateur; the closest one was *idiotes,* meaning an unskilled person, as well as an ignoramus.) Outrageous displays of wealth were inseparable from the grandeur of the Games, and every Olympiad ended with a lavish banquet for the victors, who could look forward to a future of dizzying success. An olive wreath might have been the official prize, but champions knew that the rewards were material: They would be treated like demigods around Greece, and guaranteed "sweet smooth sailing" (as the poet Pindar put it), an existence of luxury and ease, for the rest of their lives.

How could a sports fan stay away? As Epictetus observed, the daily humiliations and discomforts were a small price to pay for such a vivid experience. Or, as an athlete might put it today: "No pain, no gain."

The Ghosts of Champions Past

RE-CREATING THE ANCIENT Olympics can sometimes feel like putting together a jigsaw puzzle with most of the pieces missing. All historians of the ancient world are working with the barest shreds of a once-thriving culture. To give an idea of the loss from classical Greece, we can read today only seven of Sophocles' 113 plays, one in ten of the works of Aeschylus. When it comes to the Games, archaeologists still bicker about many of the most basic facts—the date the Olympics began, even the order of the events—let alone the finer points of the ancient Greek long-jump technique. And yet, a wonderful trove of material has survived, often by sheer luck. The official archive of ancient Olympia, for example, which included the lists of victors first compiled by Hippias of Elis and updated by Aristotle, has disappeared. But a partial copy, with the names of Olympic champions from the fifth century B.C., was found scribbled on the back of a Roman bank account.

By weaving together hundreds of such discoveries, we can re-create a vivid picture of what it must have been like to attend the Games as an athlete, a spectator, or one of the harried organizers.

The framework is, of course, ancient Olympia itself. It is now one of the most coherent of ancient Greek sites—despite the fact that it was sacked by barbarians, defiled by Christians, and finally buried in silt when local rivers flooded. For well over a millennium it remained entirely lost. It was not until 1766, when a visiting British antiquarian named Richard Chandler noticed Greek farmers plowing up marble fragments in a field, that Olympia was rediscovered. Chandler correctly identified some column bases as part of the Temple of Zeus, but it took another century for excavation to begin in earnest, by German teams sponsored by Kaiser Wilhelm Friedrich IV. A second burst of German interest came in 1936, to coincide with the Nazi Games in Berlin—the Stadium was actually unearthed on the personal commission of Hitler, who fantasized that Olympia was one site of an ancient Aryan paradise. (Relations between the German scholars and the locals of Olympia have always been amicable, and they were allowed back to the site quickly after the bitter occupation of Greece during the Second World War. Today, the Germans are still busily at work, in cooperation with the Greek Archaeological Service. Over the past century, many experts from Mainz and Munich have married locally, and every second Greek hotel owner in Olympia seems to have been christened Herman or Hilda.)

But the stones of Olympia can only communicate so much. To re-create the ancient Games, we must cast a wider net around the ancient world.

First, there are the visual sources. Greek vase paintings are far more informative than they may first seem under the harsh neon lights of museums. Almost every aspect of pagan gymnasium culture was captured on mass-produced pottery, revealing crucial data on the costumes of judges, ancient wrestling holds, and use of weights in the long jump, not to mention unexpected insights into the social background of the Olympics. We see wrestlers being thrashed for eye gouging, spectators regurgitating at banquets, young athletes being fondled by randy old men, partygoers indulging in carnal ménages. The images, taken together, create their own narrative—a flickering, almost cinematic parade of judges, strongmen, cheats, cowards, lechers, peddlers, and miscreants.

Then there are the statues. The ancient Romans were passionate about Greek art and made marble copies of the original bronzes that survive today. The museums of Berlin, Paris, New York, and London combine to create a victory banquet of ancient sportsmen, some Apolline in their sleek, idealized forms, others more realistically battered and scarred. (The original Greek images were almost all swallowed by Christian kilns. Even the "Discus Thrower," perhaps the most famous of all Western sporting images, reproduced on the coffee cups of Greek diners around the world, we know only from a copy.)

Finally, and most important, there are literary sources—ancient eyewitness reports that help reanimate the cold marble images. Thanks to the Olympics' high profile, casual references to the Games can be found scattered throughout ancient literature, turning up unexpectedly like glass tiles on the floor of the Aegean. We find them in the histories of Herodotus and Thucydides, Pliny the Elder's rambling encyclopedia, the biographies of Plutarch, the plays of Sophocles and Euripides, the soft-porn fantasies of the Roman poet Propertius. Plato refers to the Games in his political studies, Cicero in his letters, the satirist Lucian, who attended the festival at least four times, in his comic dialogues. In fact, sifting the literary archives, we sometimes have the impression that everyone in antiquity was either en route to, or coming back from, the Olympic Games.

Filling in the human details are such gems as the *Handbook for a Sports Coach,* a third-century-A.D. training manual by Philostratus, brimming with helpful advice on everything from antiperspirant dust to high-protein diets. We have the poet Pindar's victory hymns, once sung by choruses of boys at Olympic banquets; the doctor Galen prescribing an ointment for athletes' strained muscles; the historian Xenophon on the body-building regimes of Spartan girls. Most invaluable of all is an ancient travel guide to Greece, written around A.D. 160 by the antiquarian Pausanias, who made meticulous notes on Olympia's many artistic attractions—including the apocryphal tales of the original tour guides—as he went from statue to statue, stela to stela, painting to painting. Pausanias' work was so accurate that German archaeologists used it as a field guide in the 1870s.

Then there are the more exotic archaeological finds, like ancient "curse tablets," paid for by gamblers to influence chariot races—"Their horses shall be tangled in their harnesses, unable to even move!"—and a papyrus fragment discovered in a Greek town in Egypt, which contains a training drill for wrestlers ("Hold! Engage! Put your right arm around his back! Grab him by the balls!"). Even graffiti has its place, as love poems inscribed by old pederasts to the downy-cheeked youngsters grappling in the dust before them.

Slowly, the fragmented picture of the celebration begins to cohere—and we can breathe life back into the somnolent ruins of Olympia.

II

The Greek Sports Craze

To be healthy is the very best thing for anyone in life . . .
—SIMONIDES, POET, SIXTH CENTURY B.C.

AS IF IT weren't enough for the ancient Greeks to have established the foundations of Western philosophy, geometry, drama, art, and science, we can also thank them for creating our modern passion for sport. "There is no greater glory for any man alive," writes Homer in *The Odyssey,* sounding like a TV commentator on a roll, "than that which he wins by his hands and feet." The Greeks' love of competitive athletics is now securely embedded in international culture: not only our modern Olympic Games, revived in 1896 by the French baron Pierre de Coubertin, but the slew of world cups and Super Bowls, our opens and our grand slams, hark back to those energetic pagans—as does our correlating obsession with youth and the body beautiful. All of our fad diets and health magazines, our workout machines and Pilates regimes, were anticipated by the harmony-loving Greeks, whose artists devoted their lives to establishing the perfect proportion of thigh to femur. (In their admiration of physical perfection, the ancient Greeks were guiltlessly superficial. Indeed, the most enduring character of Greek mythology today may well be Narcissus.) Sport was the core of every Hellenic education; every provincial city had its gymnasium, its wrestling school, and its municipal athletic games.

It was an obsession that mystified other ancient people. "What sort of men have you brought us to fight?" a Persian general asked King Xerxes at the height of the invasion of Greece in 480 B.C. He had just learned that, while only a handful of Spartan soldiers were bravely defending Greece at the pass of Thermopylae, tens of thousands of able-bodied men were actually away at the Olympic Games, watching a wrestling final. When the general learned that the only prize was an olive wreath, he did not hide his contempt.

Why did this sports mania take such a deep hold in Greece, rather than in ancient Gaul, say, or in Libya, or Britain? It could be said that athletics combined the two vital currents of Greek life: the love of physical exercise and a rabid, relentless competitiveness.

Ancient Greece was the original Land of the Great Outdoors: thanks to the benign climate, Greeks lived *en plein air,* running through the dizzy crags of their mountainous land, swimming in the rivers and glassy blue depths of the surrounding seas. But the fragmented geography, divided by rugged valleys and inlets, also fostered divisions. Over one thousand independent states grew up around the mainland and islands, each centered on a single city, each proud of its traditions, each vying desperately for the slender natural resources of Greece. National competitiveness plunged the land into endless warfare, and was reflected within each city on a daily basis—not just in the chaotic internal politics of most states, but by the flamboyant individualism of its citizens. As Homer said, Greeks felt a personal mission "to always be the first and surpass everyone else."

Imagine the Wall Street bull pit conducted on the beach in California and you might have an idea of the abrasive male one-upmanship that emerged by the Aegean.

Greeks loved to compete over *everything*—drama, pottery, oratory, poetry reading, sculpture. Travelers held eating races in inns, doctors would vie over their surgery skills and thesis presentations. The first beauty pageants were Greek, for both males and females, as were the first kissing competitions (held in Megara, but for boys only). It was inevitable that Greeks would test one another in their most beloved pastimes.

Any excuse was good enough to hold a sports meet. The Greeks held races and athletics at weddings and at funerals. They took wagonloads of athletic equipment with them on military campaigns. And they competed at the myriad religious festivals that punctuated the annual calendar in this era before weekends. The Olympics were born from one of these cult occasions. The details are shrouded in myth: Ancient writers weighed up several contradictory tales involving gods and heroes, with the geographer Strabo wisely concluding that they were too confusing to be of any value. The current consensus of archaeologists is that Olympia had been a religious site dedicated to the Earth goddess Gaea since 1100 B.C. Some time around 1000 B.C., an agrarian festival at Olympia was combined with casual footraces dedicated to Zeus in a village atmosphere. In 776 B.C.—at least this was the date accepted by ancient tradition—the first official sports meeting was instituted at the sanctuary. We do not know precisely why Olympia's prestige grew so rapidly—it was probably thanks to Zeus's oracle there, believed to predict the result of wars—but by the sixth century B.C., the Olympic Games were regarded as the ultimate festival, towering in popularity over all other events. Held every four years to coincide with the second full moon after the summer solstice, they "attracted the best of the best, and the most celebrated of the celebrated."

A Barbarian in the Gym

A FEW OF the more sophisticated Greeks could imagine how peculiar their sports craze might seem to outsiders like Xerxes and his general. There is a hilarious dialogue written in the second century by the prolific satirist Lucian, subtitled *On Physical Exercises.* In it, a fictional barbarian prince named Anacharsis is being given a sightseeing tour of the Lyceum, one of the four great gymnasiums of Athens. As mentioned, Lucian was an inveterate sports fan—he went to the Olympic Games at least four times—but as a writer he had the unusual ability to observe his own culture with critical distance. Anacharsis—a self-confessed "good-natured barbarian"—is the original Noble Savage, and his bemused reactions might echo our own if we were somehow teleported to classical Athens. (A similar skit today might involve a Yanomamo Indian visiting a gym in New York City.)

"I'd love to know what the point of all this is," the visitor says, after he is led into the famous riverside gymnasium, where dozens of naked young men are in a courtyard, running on the spot, kicking the air or jumping back and forth to warm up. "To me, it looks like madness—these maniacs should all be locked up."

As he is escorted on, more shocking scenes unfold, involving the contact sports that were the core of the Greek phys ed curriculum. Wrestlers are murderously tossing and strangling one another, while boxers are knocking out one another's teeth.

"Why are your young men behaving so violently?" Anacharsis asks his guide, the Greek law-giver Solon. "Some of them are grappling and tripping each other—some have their hands around one another's throats—others are wallowing in pools of mud, writhing together like a herd of pigs. But the first thing the boys did when they stripped naked, I noticed, was to oil and scrape each other's bodies quite amiably, as if they were actually the best of friends. Then, something came over them—I don't know what. They put their heads down and began to push, crashing their foreheads together like angry rams.

"Look there! That young man has lifted the other one right off his legs, then dropped him on the ground like a log. . . .

"Why doesn't the official in charge put an end to this brutality? Instead, the villain seems to be encouraging them—even congratulating the one who threw the blow!"

The Greek simply chuckles condescendingly: "What is going on is called *athletics,*" he explains. Perhaps it does look a little rough, Solon admits. But wouldn't Anacharsis rather be one of these strapping young athletes, grimy, bloody-nosed, and sun-burned as they are, than a sickly, pasty-skinned bookworm—one of the sorry wretches whose bodies are "marshmallow soft, with thin blood withdrawing to the interior of the body"?

It's a question that echoes through history—reworked by Charles Atlas in advertisements, many centuries later, about the sunken-chested "90 pound weaklings" of America who have sand kicked in their faces. Indeed, the remark that helped start physical culture in the 1950s was eerily presaged by the author Philostratus in the third century A.D.: "I contend that a sunken chest should not be seen," he writes, "let alone exercised."

The Ancient Workout: A User's Guide

WHAT WAS IT like to exercise at an ancient gymnasium? It's safe to say that at every step of the way, the experience was quite different from that of the average modern health club.

In fact, the Greek gymnasium, despite the name, bears only a hazy relationship to a contemporary gym. It was less a specific building than a public sports ground, the signature feature of which was a running track. This large, open-air space was enclosed by column-lined arcades, including a covered running track for use in bad weather; it was usually placed near a river where athletes could swim, and always attached to a *palaestra,* or wrestling school. What's more, sports was only one aspect of this complex's function. The gymnasium was the ultimate Greek social center—and an exclusive male domain (only in Sparta and some other progressive Greek cities were young women given separate physical training). It was the lungs, heart, and brain of every *polis:* many had elegant gardens, parks, libraries, even, in one case in Athens, a museum of natural science. The gymnasium was where young boys of all social classes came for their primary education, where teenagers of the upper classes remained for military training, and where they generally had their first love affairs, with older men who acted as mentors. The testosterone-fueled ambiance remained addictive for older Greek men: authors often joked about "codgers" becoming figures of fun for trying to wrestle with golden-haired youngsters or join the dance classes that were a key part of education.

We can piece together the routine of an Athenian athlete preparing for the Olympics—let's call him Hippothales, a twenty-five-year-old wrestler in the mid–first century B.C. Like all Olympic hopefuls, he was obliged by the official regulations to devote himself to a training schedule in his home gymnasium for a full ten months before the start of the Games. Using the literary and archaeological evidence, we can follow Hippothales arriving at the Lyceum, the same gymnasium toured by the fictional Anarchasis.

HIPPOTHALES, DRESSED IN a tunic and carrying a pouch with his modest athletic gear, would enter the gymnasium through an antechamber flanked by impressive bronze statues of Hermes and Apollo. He makes a libation at the shrine of Hercules, patron of all athletes, then strolls along a marble arcade cluttered with artifacts—captured enemy helmets, gilt-edged shields, marble sundials, and a statuette of Eros, another Greek god who was a habitué of the gymnasium—before reaching the *apodyterion,* or undressing room. This long narrow hall looking out onto a courtyard is a hive of activity. Its stone benches are piled high with athletic apparatus—discuses in their slings, jumping weights, leather wrestling caps, blunt practice javelins—along with the occasional skinned hare an athlete may have purchased from a local hunter for dinner. It's so crowded that Hippothales has trouble even finding a space to undress. Despite the pre-Olympic hype, ordinary citizens are not kept at bay from the changing room during training sessions—the gymnasium is Athenians' piazza, their school and university rolled into one—creating the boisterous atmosphere of a social club. Old friends meet and catch up on the gossip, curious spectators gape at celebrities, self-appointed experts examine the physiques of unknown contenders. Mathematicians are at work with their students on geometrical problems, philosophers warble about the immortality of the soul or the role of athletics in an ideal society, while artists are gathered for life drawing classes. Michelangelo had to learn his anatomy from the autopsy of corpses; Greek painters and sculptors developed their brilliant skills studying athletes during their calisthenics. In fact, it feels as if all of Athens has converged on the changing room. Young boys toss knucklebones and walk their slavering hunting dogs. Fighting cocks are sparring in a corner, to the roars of gamblers. And this social melting pot is also the perfect setting for sexual

Inside the undressing room: The figure on the left *is enjoying a foot massage; the athlete in the* middle *is pouring oil from a container for his rubdown. (From an Athenian drinking cup, c. 500 B.C.)*

advances: gymnasiums are renowned pickup spots, where older men swoop on flirtatious adolescents.

Once Hippothales finds a corner, changing does not take long: his leather sandals and chiton, or light wool tunic, are flicked off in an instant. Greeks were well aware that their exercising in the nude was a unique habit, and their historians tried to explain how loincloths were abandoned. Some authors said an Athenian runner had once let his loincloth slip during a footrace and had tripped over it, prompting city elders to proclaim that all athletes should henceforth perform naked. Others thought the practice began when a runner named Orsippos of Megara decided he could race faster without it—and proved it, by winning the Olympic sprint in 720 B.C. Modern historians have tried to interpret the nudity as a throwback to ancient initiation rituals, religious cult practices, or even prehistoric hunting traditions, when men would cover themselves with oil to mask their scent. But the real answer may be more simple: Nudity appealed to the sheer exhibitionism of Greek athletes, giving them a chance to show off their physiques, and the naked male form became utterly ingrained in gym culture—in fact, the very word *gymnos* means "naked." Few cultures have been quite so shamelessly vain and superficial in their worship of physical perfection as the Greeks. Flabbiness and pale skin were subjects of derision, and vase paintings show fat boys being mocked by their peers. Whether conscious or not, the Greeks' nudity was also potently symbolic in its removal of social rank. This fact shocked other cultures as much as the Greeks' immodesty, and the fear that naked workouts would promote sexual degeneracy. Foreign aristocrats were appalled that wealthy Greeks would want to remove all signs of their social status and risk public humiliation against social inferiors. Even a larger-than-life hero like Alexander the Great, ruler of Macedonia, famously refused to take the field in athletics: He would only compete, he said, against other kings.

HIPPOTHALES DROPS HIS tunic and sandals into a basket and hangs it from a stone peg—along with his few personal belongings, probably just a flask of perfume and metal skin scraper for the baths, and his signet ring, which might injure wrestling opponents. He gives one of the attendants a bronze coin to look after his goods, since thieves commonly work the busy changing rooms. The philosopher Diogenes once ran into a shady character lurking in the shadows and quipped, "Are you here for a rubdown or a robbery?" In Athens, the penalty for these despised parasites is death. Inscriptions have been found in Roman-era baths of curses placed on clothes pilferers ("Do not allow sleep or health to him who has done me wrong. . . ."). They were taken in deadly earnest: some thieves repented when they learned they were cursed, and returned stolen goods.

After stripping down, the next stop for Hippothales is the oiling room. After water, olive oil was the most important single item in ancient Greek life, a sacred balm that had a role to play at every stage of the workout. Athletes virtually swam in the substance, basting themselves in a permanent oil slick before, during, and after exercise. At casual workouts, Hippothales would simply apply the oil himself—it was habitually poured into the left hand and rubbed over the whole body—but today he hires the gymnasium's "boy rubber" for a few coins. Later, as his Olympic training becomes more serious, coaches and professional masseurs will be poised to give him a more scientific rubdown.

Attendants pour the oil from enormous forty-gallon amphorae into bronze vats, which look like oversized punch bowls standing on three carved legs, with elegant ladles for distributions. Gymnasium-issue olive oil was of relatively low quality, produced locally by farmers in Attica, but finer oil for the table was grown on sacred trees and traded over long distances and rated like vintage wine. Vast quantities disappeared during athletics: a third of a pint per man per day was used, slightly less for boys.

Apart from its ritual importance, olive oil conserved an athlete's body moisture in the heat of the workout and functioned as a tanning lotion. While pale northern flesh fries under a layer of oil, Mediterranean skin slowly browns to the color of fired clay. Some athletes, tanned from head to foot, looked as if they had been slowly roasted on a spit; poets drooled about boys who looked "like finely-wrought bronze statues."

Happily greased, contestants in the track-and-field events could now dash outside to begin training. But Hippothales, like all others in the contact sports, had one last stop—the powder room, or *konisterion,* where he would sprinkle his body with dust. For casual bouts, wrestlers might just throw sand on one another's backs, to provide a decent grip. But the top-class competitors in Athens could choose from a colorful buffet of powders, laid out like exotic spices in wicker baskets around the room, and whose qualities for different skin types were as precisely calibrated as the unguents on sale in any California spa today. According to Philostratus, in his *Handbook for a Sports Coach,* one claylike powder was particularly good for opening the pores, another an excellent antiperspirant for oily complexions. A terracotta powder repaired dry skin, while a yellow dust provided the most becoming sheen—"a delight to see on a body in good shape." These powders had to be applied evenly, Philostratus stresses—"sprinkled with a fluid motion of the wrist and with fingers spread apart. The dust should fall more in a gentle shower than a thunder burst, so that it covers the athlete's body like soft down." Hippothales pays careful attention to the process, since aesthetics have always been crucial in Greek sports. Good health may have been the best thing in life, as Simonides said, but the next best thing (the poet hastily added) was "to be handsome."

Jump to the Flutes

HIPPOTHALES IS NOW ready for his warm-up exercises, many of which are performed to music. Greeks loved to combine

Boxers doing warm-up exercises to flute music. (From a Greek amphora, c. 400 B.C.)

the harmony of the body with the rhythms of instruments, creating an incipient form of aerobics. He can drift from one group to another. In open spaces, some athletes are swinging lead weights like dumbbells back and forth to the accompaniment of flutes made from the shinbones of stags. Some troupes march on their toes, jump on the spot, or leap up and kick their buttocks with their heels, all to hypnotic, high-pitched tunes. (In Sparta, where girls could train, one woman claimed on her memorial that she did this last exercise one thousand times.)

We can get an idea of the more rigorous exercise regimes Hippothales might have pursued from an ancient self-help book called *How to Stay Healthy,* written by the illustrious physician Galen in the second century. The good doctor systematically prescribes chapters on exercises for the legs, arms, and abdomen, each of which is broken down into three subsets: *controlled exercises* for muscle tone, *quick exercises* for speed, and *violent exercises* for strength. In the first group, athletes were advised to carry heavy weights, climb ropes, or extend their arms while their companions tried to pull them down. Quick exercises included rolling back and forth on the ground, running in ever-decreasing circles, and standing on tiptoe and rapidly moving one's arms up and down. Violent exercises were the same, only using weights and done more vigorously. Runners, for example, would put on increasing amounts of armor as they sprinted along the sacred track.

What was the training for specific sports? We know that boxers converged on a room hung with punching bags, which were made from animal skins stuffed with grain, sand, or fig seeds, then hung from the rafters like pendulous smoked hams. Shadowboxing was extremely popular, and was also a hit with the admiring crowds at training sessions, shouting their support as if a real match were in progress. For Hippothales, a wrestler, the training regime is more structured. We have a good idea of his probable drill, thanks to the survival of a unique shred of papyrus from a do-it-yourself manual found in Oxyrhynchus, an obscure Greek colony in Egypt. (Vulnerable to moisture, most papyri disintegrated over time; some 70 percent of our surviving papyri come from a garbage dump in this town by the Nile, where the bone-dry sands have preserved them through the centuries.) The document lists a series of practice holds and throws, which a wrestling instructor is barking out to his students: "You, put your right arm around his back! You, take an under-hold. You, step across and engage! You, turn around! You, grip him by the balls!"

For Hippothales, the day's training may wind down with a relaxing game of handball—which Galen called "the most satisfactory, all-round exercise." Every gymnasium had an enclosed court, where athletes would hit a small leather ball back and forth to themselves, often for hours, to build up their arm strength. Another, more social game, *hapastum,* involved two or more men throwing a ball over the head of a player in the middle, who tried to intercept it either by jumping or wrestling the other players to the ground. The author Athenaeus describes the genial atmosphere: "A player seized the ball and passed it with a laugh . . . amid resounding shouts of 'out of bounds,' 'too far,' 'right beside him,' 'over his head,' 'on the ground,' 'up in the air,' 'too short,' 'pass it back in the scrimmage.' " The Lyceum of Athens, like other gymnasiums, actually employed a specialist to manage ball play, but we know surprisingly little about what games were popular. Athenian reliefs show athletes bouncing balls on their thighs—looking like today's soccer stars—and using racquets strung with animal gut to hit a ball against a wall, like an early version of lacrosse. *Urania,* or "sky ball," involved someone tossing a ball to a crowd of athletes who jumped up to catch it, like modern basketball players leaping for a rebound.

But what about team ball games? Did Homer play rugby? It was a question, oddly enough, that British historians once seriously considered, hoping beyond hope that their favorite team games had classical origins. "Shall we one day discover a representation of Greek boys playing football?" pined the academic Norman Gardiner in 1930. "The Chinese certainly played football at an early date: the Italians of the Middle Ages had their game of Calzio. . . ." He pointed out that both the Greeks and the Romans had an air-filled ball called the *follis,* and it seems inconceivable that someone, somewhere, wouldn't have thought to give it a kick. "For the present we do not know," Gardiner sighs; "we can only hope for future discoveries." Today, we are still waiting. The only genuine team game we have any evidence for in the ancient era was developed by the Spartans. It was called *episkyros* and was played in a large field marked with white stones. The rules are obscure, but it's clear that two teams tossed a small leather ball back and forth, trying to drive each other back over their defense line. With its aerial to-and-fro and bone-crunching collisions, one historian has compared it with American football played without rules, helmets, or padding. But the game never took off in the rest of Greece.

Tyrants of the Sports Ground

Sharpening an athlete who is naturally excellent
A trainer, with the guiding hand of a god
Can rouse him to enormous fame.
— ANONYMOUS, C. 450 B.C.

IN THE SIXTH century B.C., the teenage Milo of Croton developed his own rustic weight-training program on a farm in southern Italy by lifting a young bull calf every day until the beast was fully grown. Bulked up on this natural Nautilus machine, the original Italian Stallion went on to become the greatest of all Olympic wrestling champions, winning the boys' event in 540 B.C. and five successive wrestling Olympiads over twenty years—a record never broken in the nearly twelve centuries of the Games.

But most Olympics hopefuls like Hippothales, more pragmatically, hired private trainers. These professionals, called *paidotribai,* were key figures in the ancient Greek sporting culture, and their services were never more in demand than during the ten-month training period that athletes were obliged to embark on before the Olympic Games. They were usually retired athletes themselves, over forty years old, with practical experience of anatomy, nutrition, medicine, and physiotherapy. The typical coach was rough and poorly educated: some were barely able to sign their own names. But many were sophisticated specialists with their own elaborate exercise programs, or rich men with an abiding passion for sport—or thirst for fame. Reflected glory was potent. The names of top trainers were bound forever with athletes who won the olive wreath at Olympia, recorded on memorials and repeated in hymns. Coaches joined in all the Olympic ceremonies and had a special section in the Stadium;

they sat by a champion's side at the victory banquets and would walk beside him in triumphal processions. Later, they could publicize their techniques—even write their own training manuals.

Some of these celebrity trainers were marvelous characters, whose morale-boosting powers were legendary. At the Olympics of 520 B.C., the boxer Glaucus was about to admit defeat when his trainer bellowed, "Give him one for the plough!"—a reference to the day when Glaucus first proved his strength as a teenager on a farm by straightening a bent ploughshare with his bare hands. The young man apparently bucked up, and with one massive blow felled his opponent like a tree. Other trainers took the adage "Death or victory" to heart. A wrestler named Arrhichion was being choked and was about to raise his finger in surrender, until his trainer yelled, "Oh, what a beautiful epitaph! He never gave up at Olympia"—an echo of a military axiom praising those who never surrender. Arrhichion, inspired by these touching words, fought to the death. Another unnamed coach was so exasperated when one of his wrestlers *did* attempt to surrender that he rushed forward and stabbed the athlete with a sharp metal instrument, killing him. The coach of Promachus of Pellene used more subtle psychology. Learning that his young charge was desperately in love, the coach pretended that the girl had promised her favors if Promachus emerged victorious at Olympia. Thrilled by this fabricated promise, Promachus won the *pankration* in 404 B.C. against overwhelming odds.

While many coaches developed their own "scientific" training programs, it was Iccus of Tarentum, an Olympic pentathlon champion in 444 B.C., who was the first to take the next step and write his own textbook. It has disappeared—all we know about it is that it called for moderation in training and diet—but an army of other celebrity athletes followed suit with treatises, written on papyrus scrolls and copied by teams of slaves for booksellers around the Mediterranean. These various ancient training manuals, which once numbered in the hundreds, are the unrecognized antecedents of *Buns of Steel, Super Abs,* and *Total Fitness in Only Two Weeks!*

Philostratus' famous *Handbook for a Sports Coach,* penned in the third century A.D., was found by accident in an archive near Constantinople in 1844, lost, then rediscovered at an Ottoman manuscript sale fifty years later. Showing us the breadth of trainers' interests, it includes specialized massages to offset overeating, exercise to treat alcohol abuse, and how to identify an athlete's personality by his eye color. It explains how to deal with anxiety, insomnia, anemia, excessive perspiring, or the debilitating effects of sex. (Mainly through self-restraint: "What sort of man," the author asks, "would rather succumb to shameful pleasures than enjoy the wreaths and proclamations of Sacred Heralds?" Those plagued by "habitual nightly emissions" are prescribed special workouts.) The reader learns that it is much healthier to sunbathe when the wind is blowing from the north, when the sun's rays are "pure and beneficial." And there is considerable arcane discussion of how to balance the four humors of the body, which were the basis of all ancient medicine. (The ideal athletic temperament was "warm and moist," the author intones, and thus more obedient—"free from dregs, impurities, and excessive secretions are those in whom the stream of phlegm and gall is scanty.") Philostratus also rails against the overly theoretical training systems that were plaguing Greek athletics. All ancient intellectuals loved abstract formulas—which led to some bizarre fitness regimes. Even Athenian philosophers invented exercise programs, despite the fact that they had no practical experience. (Which sport created morally upright citizens? they wondered.)

In Philostratus' day, one popular program called the tetrad system involved an unbreakable four-day athletic cycle, with the second day devoted to extreme training, almost to the point of physical collapse. Its rigidity claimed casualties: having won the Olympic wreath for wrestling in A.D. 209, a Greek-Egyptian champion named Gerentus went off on a celebratory drinking binge. He returned to the gymnasium complaining of a filthy hangover, but his trainer would not permit any break in his grueling regime. In mid-practice, Gerentus dropped dead from a heart attack. Travelers could see his gravestone on the highway outside Athens, warning posterity of the dangers of inflexibility.

Many Greek doctors were appalled at the proliferation of these pseudoscientific manuals and tried to denounce them. The famous Galen acidly pointed out that author-trainers were often failed athletes—half-educated men profiting from the ignorance and gullibility of wannabe champions. He argued that their overspecialized and excessive exercise regimes were doing more harm than good, producing a brutish race of Greek athletes who were both doltish and ugly, their froglike bodies distorted and ill-proportioned. But he had little hope in the war of words. Trainers remained paramount in the gymnasium, and the Greek public's appetite for fad theories insatiable—especially when it came to diet.

FROM EARLIEST ANTIQUITY, what a top athlete should *consume* was considered as important as his exercise regime, and Hippothales' trainer would have come up with a detailed meal plan.

According to nostalgic tradition, the first Olympians shared the simple, balanced diet of the average Greek, supping on thick vegetable soup, bread, cheese, olives, fruit, and honeyed cakes. All that changed when a certain Dromeus of Stymphalos won two footraces at Olympia in 480 B.C. on an all-meat diet. High-protein meals became all the rage—a source of resentment for ordinary Greeks, who could not afford expensive meat. Wrestlers and boxers began to gorge on beef, pork, and lamb, becoming (as the playwright Euripides put it) "the slaves of their jaws and the victims of their bellies."

Fad diets proliferated. Learned dieticians would debate which fish were healthier, those from the swamps or deep-sea fish? Were fish that ate seaweed better for you, or fish that ate algae? Some advocated pork—provided the pigs had been fed on cornel berries or acorns. Swine raised by the sea were injurious to health; those brought up by rivers were even worse "because they may have fed on crabs." (Savvy coaches did not just pay attention to what was on the plate, advising their charges to avoid intelligent conversation at mealtimes, as it would spoil their digestion and give them headaches; they also weighed in on the style of after-dinner belching.) Ideas for extreme diets came from all quarters. Charmis of Sparta, an Olympic sprinting champion in 688 B.C., espoused eating nothing but dried figs. Xenophon advised athletes to avoid all bread, the first nonyeast diet in history. The Pythagoreans forbade their athletes to touch beans— but Galen recommended a high-bean diet for gladiators, provided the beans were properly boiled to avoid flatulence. Hippocrates considered cheese to be a "wicked food," despite the fact that it was supposedly the staple of superhuman Homeric heroes. In the end, much like today's diet fads, Greek dietary recommendations were so contradictory as to be meaningless.

The Joy of Steam

WHEN THE DAY'S training is over, our exhausted Hippothales, caked with dust and sand, heads for the bathhouse, where fountains spout hot and cold water from lion-head faucets. Several streams usually poured out at head height, like modern showers, into basins, buckets, and hip baths. Once again, olive oil was the all-purpose lotion: athletes used it as the basis for soap and shampoo during bathing, mixing it with detergent powder (they could choose from a lye made of ashes, a fine-grained clay, or an alkali called *litron*). The sticky blend was then scraped off the skin with the strigil or *stlengis*—a bronze tool in

One athlete washing another after a workout. (From a Greek drinking cup, c. 475 B.C.)

the shape of a crescent moon. But even after rinsing, an athlete's muscles went without olive oil only for a second: the sacred liquid was quickly reapplied by masseurs, mixed in with a few drops of perfume distilled from flowers as a deodorant.

Some Greek moralists denounced the pampering of the bathhouse for breeding weakness and sloth. They sanctimoniously recalled the days of Homeric heroes, who washed only in wild rivers no matter what the season. Few athletes seemed to agree. The Romans took personal hygiene to a higher level and in the first century A.D. introduced to Greece their far more elaborate *thermae,* or heated baths, each with a trio of steam rooms and deep pools of varying temperatures. In Athens, they erected vast bathing complexes for both men and women, which combined the sport functions of the Greek gymnasium with restaurants, bars, libraries, and even special booths for prostitutes.

WE CAN NOW leave our athlete Hippothales in the bathhouse and return to Anacharsis, the Noble Savage of Lucian's dialogue, on his tour of the Lyceum. To the barbarian, Solon's explanations of the Greek gym culture oscillate between the baffling and the downright comical. But when Anacharsis learns about the Olympic Games, the idea that multitudes of Greeks gather to simply *watch* athletics seems the most incredible fact of all. "I feel sorry for the athletes, but even more for the spectators. You tell me the most important people in Greece love to watch sport. But how can they waste their time on such frivolity? It can't be that they actually *enjoy* seeing this sort of thing—people being hit and beaten up, dashed to the ground and being beaten to a pulp! In my country, if one citizen strikes another, he faces criminal charges, even if there are only a couple of witnesses—let alone the thousands that gather at your vast Olympic Games." And athletes who endure this public degradation, he scoffs questioningly, are considered "equal to the gods"?

The guide Solon, sounding a little exasperated, says that Anacharsis will change his mind when he goes to the great Games himself. When he immerses himself in the atmosphere, joins the cheering crowd, sees the athletes' strength and skill, he "won't be able to stop applauding."

III.

Countdown

> - *Plastering the dressing room in the Gymnasium:*
>   16 *drachmae (Paid to Pasion).*
> - *Weeding and rolling the Stadium running track:*
>   21 *drachmae (Paid to Smyrnaios).*
> - *Digging and leveling the long-jump pits:*
>   220 *drachmae (Paid to Smyrnaios).*
>
> —FROM THE FINANCIAL ACCOUNT FOR PREPARING THE
> GAMES AT DELPHI, 246 B.C.

EVERY FOURTH SPRING, a trio of sacred heralds were sent out from Elis—the city within whose domain the sanctuary of Olympia lay—to announce the date of the upcoming Games of Zeus. For the Greeks, the arrival of one of these flamboyantly uniformed officials must have been anticipated as a colorful seasonal rite. A herald's theatrical figure would have been easy to spot at a distance as he picked his way on mule-back through the pastures and river valleys: his robes were royal purple, his head crowned with olive wreaths, and he carried the sacred banner, or caduceus, a staff carved with a pair of copulating snakes used by wing-footed Hermes, messenger of the gods. In his satchel was the schedule for the Games. The date was determined by a complex formula to ensure that the middle day of the five-day festival coincided with the second full moon after the summer solstice. This meant that the Games were usually held in August or early September—the summer lull that came after the annual harvest but before the picking of the olives.

The three heralds, or *spondophoroi,* were enjoying one of history's first great travel junkets: hopping separately around mainland Greece and the Aegean islands, they were treated like kings at every step. The hospitality began the moment a herald arrived at a new city's gates and was met by the local *proxenos*—the official representative of Elis. The visitor would be bathed, then feast on the finest local delicacies and regional wines. The next day, he would be taken before the city council or assembly, where he would be received with great respect as he read in ringing tones the invitation to the upcoming Games, and the terms of the sacred Olympic Truce. Then came a fine state dinner.

This Olympic Truce was one of the ancient world's most extraordinary traditions. It imposed an armistice across the land—an almost enchanted ban on the Greeks' incessant feuding—whose terms were enforced by Zeus himself. During this sacred peace, no military attacks could be made, no judicial cases conducted, nor death penalties carried out. The main purpose was to ensure the safety of athletes and spectators on their journeys to the Games, and to keep the entire district of Elis sacrosanct during the festival. Originally the peace was enforced for one month on either side of the Games, but when visitors started to come from farther afield, from Greek colonies in Italy and Asia Minor, the period was extended to two months. (Remoter cities, far-flung islands, and Greek colonies around the Mediterranean were probably alerted by letter.) Its terms had originally been defined in 776 B.C. for the first Games and inscribed in concentric circles onto a hefty golden discus, which still hung in pride of place in the Temple of Hera at Olympia. And despite some notorious exceptions, the truce was honored.

The heralds generally arrived at least two months before the date of the Games: the sixty-day countdown to the Olympics had officially begun. But for the Olympics organizers themselves—a bevy of provincial aristocrats in the city of Elis—the planning process had gotten under way long before. The festival may have been only five days long. It may have felt to some visitors like little more than inspired chaos. But it was nonetheless the result of elaborate behind-the-scenes organization, without which it would have collapsed entirely. The athletics facilities had to be prepared; judges had to be trained; sponsorship had to be arranged; catering needed to be planned.

Running the Games was a full-time job.

The Hereditary Hosts

FEW PEOPLE TODAY have even heard of the city of Elis. Its ancient ruins, which lie forty miles northeast of Olympia, are now the merest rubble; even in antiquity, it was essentially a sleepy rural outpost. And yet it was the Elians who were the official stewards, for generation after generation, of the illustrious Olympic Games.

This tight-knit coterie of landowners, whose wealth came from cattle- and horse-breeding, might seem an unlikely group to be running the greatest festival of the ancient world, but they held their position through unshakeable Greek tradition. It was King Iphitos of Elis who had first declared the Games in 776 B.C., acting on divine instructions. Greece at the time was wracked by plague and warfare, and in desperation Iphitos had consulted the Delphic oracle. He was told that the only way to end the curse was to celebrate athletic games at Olympia, forty miles from his city. Iphitos did so, and the pestilence disappeared. In the centuries that followed, the ruling class of Elians drew from their own ranks the Olympic judges and micromanaged every aspect of the festival.

Luckily, the Elians seem to have been a sophisticated, well-educated, and capable clique, who by the classical era had devel-

A laborer levels the running track. (Adapted from the interior of a Greek drinking cup, c. 425 B.C.)

oped an efficient sporting bureaucracy. There was an all-powerful Olympic Council, made up of two dozen cattle barons with time on their hands, which oversaw the whole festival and made broad decisions on scheduling or adding new events. There was a commission of law codifiers, who passed on the rules from generation to generation. But the most visible and active officials at each Games were the ten Olympic judges—loftily called *Hellanodikai*, Greek guardians of the law—whose responsibilities were far broader than those of any Olympic judge today.

These ten *über*-judges would not only adjudicate at sporting events but help organize the day-to-day operation of the Games and even supervise the final training of Olympic competitors. Their duties were divided: three judges were chosen to preside over the equestrian events, three the pentathlon, and three all the other events, while the tenth judge coordinated their efforts. During the festival itself, they could impose fines or order whippings, and all of their decisions were final; only an appeal to the Olympic Council could overturn them, a move no athlete would take lightly. From the time of their selection ten months before the Games, these top officials were permitted to swan about Elis dressed, like the Olympic heralds, in robes of royal purple, a costume that paid honor to King Iphitos, who was sole judge at the first Games. The social jockeying for the jobs must have been intense. Aristocrats all, they were selected from among the Elian ruling class by a complicated, and no doubt contentious, mix of voting and random lot. The position was a valued honor, despite the fact that it was time-consuming, unpaid, and extremely costly. *Hellanodikai* often found themselves using their own funds to cover unexpected incidentals like hiring extra groundsmen or buying new robes for the priests.

Although the impartiality of the Olympic judges was legendary, the fact that Elians could also compete in the Games did raise the occasional ancient eyebrow. In the tight-knit community of Elis, a judge might well see his own friends or relatives taking the field. Even more strangely, the judges *themselves* were technically allowed to compete, by entering their own horses in the equestrian events. According to Herodotus, envoys from Elis were sent in 590 B.C. to Egypt, the source of ancient wisdom, asking for advice on tightening up the Olympic rules. The shaven-headed Pharaoh reviewed the regulations and pronounced that, for the judging to be completely fair and avoid all taint of partisanship, Elian citizens should not be allowed to participate as athletes. The envoys politely thanked the Pharaoh for his sage advice but never took it. Still, scandals were remarkably rare. For the most part, the Elian judges were respected and admired, and the Olympics had a reputation as the "cleanest" of all Greek competitions. As one approving Greek sports fan remarked, the Elian officials behaved "as if they were on trial as much as the Olympic athletes, anxious not to commit any errors."

From Cow Paddock to Stadium

AT LEAST IN one respect, running the Games was easier in the ancient world than the modern. Whereas today the setting for the Olympics traverses the globe—with each host city accepting a new crush of logistical problems to prepare for the extravaganza—the original festival was always held at the same verdant spot. In Olympia, a compact religious sanctuary some forty miles from the host city Elis, the Greek Games had a permanent home for 293 successive Olympics.

Physically, the site was strikingly beautiful—exuding (as one historian put it) "a peaceful charm that we rarely feel in that land of rugged mountains." Some two dozen marble buildings stood in a fertile alluvial plain, bordered by pine-covered hills to the north, the river Alpheus to the south, and the river Cladeus to the west. The sanctuary's core, the Sacred Grove of Zeus, was surprisingly small: known to Greeks as the Altis, it was a walled-off enclosure that covered a mere six acres. But it was the greatest pilgrimage center of the pagan world, thanks to three famous temples, dedicated to Zeus, his consort Hera, and his mother, Rhea. Scattered haphazardly in between these edifices were some seventy altars covering the Greek pantheon, the grave of the hero Pelops, and a jumble of statues, memorials, shrines, and civic monuments. The spiritual life of this serene outpost carried on without interruption in the four years between Games, with a staff of around fifty, including (one inscription tells us) three priests, a flutist, a wine pourer, a keeper of the keys, a butcher-cook, and a tour guide catering to a few pious pilgrims and sightseers.

Lovely, Olympia certainly was—but as a venue for a mass gathering, it certainly had its disadvantages. Not only was it in a remote rural area, with an almost total lack of accommodation, but the sporting facilities were surprisingly rudimentary and fell into disrepair in the long period between events. A wrestling school had been built on the fringe of the Sacred Grove in the third century B.C., but the Gymnasium was not added until the first century A.D.; before that date, athletes merely worked out in the fields. A Stadium and horse-racing track lay to the east of the temple complex, but they were not maintained during the off-season; in fact, they were used by local villagers to pasture their sheep and cattle. Hammered by winter rains and baked by summer sun, their banks became overgrown with shrubbery and their tracks uneven. To bring the facilities up to par, every fourth year saw an urgent flurry of spring cleaning at Olympia, and the dreamy torpor of the sanctuary was shattered by an army of workers giving the whole environment a top-to-bottom polish.

Teams of laborers made the forty-mile trip from Elis, leading their mule-drawn wagons along a purpose-built highway, paved with smooth stone and grooved in double ruts for wheels. Heavy supplies such as sacks of fresh white earth and mortar would have been barged the fifteen miles upriver from the west coast of the Peloponnese. Extra hands could be cheaply hired from the many asylum seekers at Olympia—refugees had the right to stay at any Greek sanctuary until their legal matters were settled. Elian artisans, whose skills and experience at Olympia had been passed down from generation to generation, pitched tents in the surrounding fields to create a workers' camp. In the warm spring sunshine, they began to hoe up the wrestling grounds, lay down fresh white sand, level the running tracks, and dig new pits for the long jump and wells for water.

An inscription found at Delphi, dating from 246 B.C., gives luminous insight into how Greek athletic sites were prepared; it lists laborers' fees for Delphi's own prestigious Pythian Games, which were held in different summers from the Olympics. (A modern historian has ingeniously converted the rates into today's currency, by comparing the cost of olive oil then and today. An amphora of forty liters is known to have cost eighteen drachmas in ancient Athens, while one liter of olive oil today is worth about US $10 in a supermarket. Thus a drachma was worth about $22 in our terms, although when making the comparison it should be kept in mind that a skilled Greek artisan in the time of Pericles was paid only one drachma or $22 a day.) The Greeks' matter-of-fact professionalism and attention to detail would be manifest in work at Olympia:

- Digging and rolling the practice running track in the Gymnasium: $814 (Paid to Agazalos).
- Repairs to the Stadium entrance: $566 (Paid to Euthydamos).
- Repair to the wall by the shrine of the goddess Demeter: $1,298 (Paid to Kleon).
- Construction of 36 turning posts for the running track: $528 (Paid to Anazagoras).
- Cleaning out and fencing the Kastalian spring with the Gorgon's head spout: $396 (Paid to Kleon).
- 270 bushels of white earth for covering the covered practice track @ $6.42 per bushel: $1,732.50 (Paid to Agazalos).

In Olympia, which was filled with ancient statuary, art specialists were shipped in to oversee restoration work. Precious metals were given new luster, the colored pediments of the temples retouched. The lion-head waterspouts ringing the roof of the Temple of Zeus often had to be replaced: there were 102 of these once-gracious design features—they were used to drain rainwater in winter—but because they were so heavy, they tended to snap off. Local villagers, meanwhile, rubbed fresh olive oil onto the forty-foot-high statue of Zeus to protect its valuable ivory from moisture. (The workers were known as the Burnishers, and were believed to be descendants of the statue's original artist, Phidias. They could only do so much. By the second century A.D., when the icon was over five hundred years old, visitors reported that the statue's framework had become infested with rodents, and that their squeaks were becoming a distraction to the pious.)

Catering, meanwhile, was put in the hands of private enterprise. Olympia was situated in a sparsely populated rural area, so

Greek artisans repair statues in a workshop. (From a Greek drinking cup,
c. 380 B.C.)

itinerant vendors flocked there to provide for the captive market.
These vendors were required to have licenses, and the Elians appointed a commissioner of marketers to impose on-the-spot fines
for shoddy merchandise or price gouging. Merchants came to
oversee the construction of their booths and bring teams of livestock to be penned for sacrifices and banquets. Local farmers sup-
plied the wood, and the air was filled with the sounds of
carpentry.

The festival was taking shape—and it resembled a sprawling
fairground. But impressive as it was, this hive of activity was still
considered secondary.

The real buzz was back in the city of Elis, where, a full month
before the Games, the hopeful athletes had begun to arrive.

IV.

The Olympic Boot Camp

You say you want to be an Olympic champion. But wait. Think about what is involved. . . . You will have to hand your body over to your coach just as you would to a doctor. You will have to obey every instruction. You will have to give up sweet desserts, and eat only at fixed times, no matter how hot or cold the weather. You will be forbidden to drink chilled water. Even wine will be limited. Then, in the contests, you must gouge and be gouged. There will be times that you will sprain a wrist, twist your ankle, swallow mouthfuls of sand and be flogged. And even after all that, you will probably lose!

—EPICTETUS, STOIC PHILOSOPHER, FIRST CENTURY A.D.

BY THE FIRST full moon after the summer solstice—thirty days before the Games began—every athlete who wanted to compete in the Olympics was obliged to register personally before the judges in the city of Elis. It was this host city rather than the sanctuary of Olympia that became the original Olympic Village, where an invasion of hopefuls were forced to train together in isolation throughout the midsummer. To a modern sportsman, this tradition might seem counterproductive, even downright sadistic: Athletes who had already been working for nine

The rigors of training. As two pankratiasts *struggle on the ground, a judge steps in to stop an eye-gouging, wielding his stick to punish the offender. (From an Athenian drinking cup, c. 480 B.C.)*

months with their private coaches suddenly had to submit to an alien regime, renowned throughout Greece for its pseudomilitary rigor, full of petty disciplines and humiliating punishments. But its practical purpose was to weed out the weaker athletes, until only the best of the best were left to compete in the final events at Olympia. And the harshness was also symbolic: it was through this domination period that the Elians confirmed their absolute control over the upcoming festival. Athletes accepted the system, usually arriving with a support group of their fathers and brothers, the rich with their entourage of servants and masseurs. Trainers tagged along, but stayed quiet on the sidelines: They could be flogged for questioning the Elian exercise programs.

New arrivals at Elis observed a pleasant, if not unusually strik-ing, provincial city surrounded by rich farmland. In the second century A.D., the ancient travel-guidebook writer Pausanias summed up its attractions in a few paragraphs, noting that it had little to offer in the way of fine art or splendid buildings. But Elis's drowsy atmosphere would be quickly shattered by the in-flux of pumped-up athletes. We have no records of the numbers that would arrive before each Olympiad, but with over seven hundred city-states in mainland Greece and 250 Greek colonies around the Mediterranean, it's easy to imagine eight hundred adult athletes converging for the eighteen competitions, plus a support army of grooms, servants, masseurs, family members, and trainers. Around two hundred teenagers competing in the boys' events would have swelled the numbers. The atmosphere in Elis must have been riotous—especially since the marketplace in the city center was cleared for use as a practice horse track. The aristocrats of Elis were famous for their stud farms, and they hap-pily joined visitors galloping bareback on horses and speeding their painted chariots past the elegant temples in a frenzy of machismo from dawn until dusk.

For newcomers, the first order of business was to present themselves to the ten Olympic judges and declare in which events they wished to compete. The procedure occurred at a building called the Hellanodikaion—connected by a private road to the gymnasiums, this had been the judges' office and home for ten months as they were tutored in the rules by higher officials. Each athlete had to demonstrate that he was the legiti-mate son of free-born Greek parents, that he had not committed murder or sacrilege, and that he was registered on the citizen ros-ter of his native city. "Greekness" was sometimes a delicate mat-ter: A poor fisherman from Argos might walk through the inspection easily, because of his undeniably Greek heritage, but nobles from remoter parts of the world sometimes had to resort to complex genealogical arguments or even cite lines from Homer to prove that their hometown had legendary Greek links.

After Greece was conquered by Macedonia in 338 B.C. and then the Romans in 146 B.C., the judges pragmatically became more flexible in their definition, allowing anyone who *spoke* Greek to compete.

Athletes were permitted to change their home citizenship for the Olympics—and even accept money to do so. Sotades of Crete, for example, a long-distance winner in 380 B.C., took cold cash to compete as an Ephesian in the next Games. (The practice may have been legal, but it certainly did not endear Sotades to his home island: the Cretans, incensed, banished him, turned his home into a prison, and tore down a bronze memorial to his past victories.) Blatant lying to the judges, however, could be severely punished. A Spartan who claimed he was Boeotian to escape an embargo on his countrymen in 420 B.C. was publicly flogged.

Latecomers who arrived after the cutoff date had to present a valid excuse, like illness or shipwreck. In A.D. 93, an Alexandrian boxer—charmingly nicknamed "the Sprinkler" for his ability to spray his opponents' blood around the ring—told the judges that his boat's sailing had been delayed by unfavorable winds. The judges were ready to accept this fib until another boxer named Heraclides swore that he had recently seen the Sprinkler signing on for prizefights in Asia Minor. The Sprinkler was disqualified, but nursed a grudge: He later rushed Heraclides and thumped him to the ground. The judges then levied a hefty fine against him for "dishonoring the Games."

IT'S EASY TO imagine the excitement for first-time contestants arriving at the famous gyms of Elis. They had three to choose from: the so-called Old Gymnasium, with its adjoining wrestling school and venerable hundred-foot room; the Square Gymnasium, with a sacred running track; and the so-called Soft Gymnasium, named for its pliable floor.

Although there were far more magnificent sports complexes in Greece, let alone the luxurious spas of Asia Minor, nothing could quite compare with the hallowed Elian gymnasiums in the countdown to the Olympic Games. We can imagine the scene on a hot day in mid-July, two weeks into the mandatory training regime. The cream of Greek manhood would be present, parading their buffed physiques, their short beards trimmed to a point. Some would be running up and down the track, others tossing the discus and javelin in designated ranges or swimming in the shady river nearby. In the wrestling school, strongmen in skullcaps were sparring in the courtyard, their grunts echoing through the air. Attendants would be tilling the area set aside for the *pankration* with picks, and watering it to create a soft mud that would cushion the brutal throws. The aura of tradition lay heavy in the air, reinforced by the gaze of statues of Olympic champions—heroes like Milo of Croton and Theagenes of Thasos, probably the two most famous of all ancient Greek athletes, each of whom had trained on this very spot.

What sort of men had made it to the fields of Elis? The ancient Greeks kept no statistics, but we can put together a profile of Olympic contenders from victory lists, inscriptions, and literary sources. They came, we know, from every corner of the Greek world—representing themselves first as individuals, and placing less emphasis on their homeland than do modern athletes. They also came from a wide cross-section of society. Like basketball in American ghettoes and soccer in British slums, athletics was one of the great motors of social mobility in ancient Greece: the son of a dirt-poor fishmonger might, in certain circumstances, be plucked from obscurity and reach celestial heights of fame.

In 416 B.C., the snobbish young aristocrat Alcibiades famously complained that the Games were being flooded by lower-class riffraff. But the underlying democratic process of Greek athletics had been present ever since the Olympics' birth. The first recorded victor in the Games of 776 B.C.—which had only a single event, the 210-yard sprint—was a cook named Coroibos. For the next two centuries, aristocrats largely dominated the Games—they were the only ones who had the leisure time to train, and the spare cash to visit Olympia—but the chroniclers still record victories by goatherds and farm boys. By the classical era (c. 480–320 B.C.), the massive popularity of the Olympics had widened the social net: Greek cities, to promote their own prestige, voted stipends to athletes who showed promise, or even paid for a young man's personal trainer and travel expenses to reach the festival. Private patrons set up bursaries, and athletic guilds began to develop a system of scholarships; there is evidence that athletes were paid per diems of several drachmas a day during their monthlong training session at Elis, to help defray the cost of competing at the Olympics. In fact, few other high-ranking Greek sportsmen shared Alcibiades' disdain for poor athletes. The scions of wealthy families continued to fill the Olympic rosters, despite the possibility that they could find themselves grappling with the son of an olive merchant rather than a fellow member of the "gilded youth."

In the gymnasiums of Elis, for rich and poor it would be a sobering month: in a short time, the number of applicants would be trimmed, as the grueling trials eliminated the weakest.

The Selection Process

FOR SOME, THE path to Olympia had begun even before they were born. It was known that if a pregnant woman dreamed she was giving birth to an eagle, then her son was surely destined to become a successful athlete. If a father dreamed he was eating his son's shoulder, then he would profit from his son's wrestling career. If he was devouring his son's feet, logically, the family would make a fortune from his running.

In fact, the whole of Greek life, it could be said, was geared toward the production of Olympic athletes. For those who made it to Elis, the process had probably begun at the tender age of six, when they had first begun their schooling and come to the attention of the *gymnastes*—the ancient phys-ed teacher who worked in every city gymnasium. The initial trial by fire would have been at a local sports meeting, during a religious festival. The scouting was slightly more haphazard in rural areas of Greece. Theagenes of Thasos was revealed as Olympic material at age nine, when he heaved a giant bronze statue in the village market onto his shoulder and carried it off. Instead of having the boy executed for impiety, the village elders sent their superboy off to wrestling school.

We can pretty well map out a standard career path. Most Greek festivals lavished victors with money and presents, which allowed a rising young sports star to support himself entirely by athletics. A hopeful might start out picking up the relatively modest prizes at local events, and saving enough to travel to the more prominent and lucrative annual games in a great city like Megara, Boeotia, or Athens. Awards in Athens, for example, totaled an estimated US $600,000 in today's terms. A teenager who won the sprint took home fifty amphorae of olive oil, which he was then able to sell (a hefty haul, today worth perhaps $45,000); the winner of the men's footrace racked up twice that. Wealthy cities in Asia Minor like Ephesus and Pergamum would offer enough for a victor to buy a small villa. There were over two hundred of these so-called prize games, which provided material awards, around 150 B.C.—under the Romans, the numbers doubled—and professional athletes could accrue vast private fortunes touring the Mediterranean from one high-budget event to the next.

The next level for athletes were the Sacred Games—the Big Four, held one per summer in rotation. Three of these four national events, at Nemea, Delphi, and Corinth, were on a par in prestige; they awarded symbolic wreaths of celery, laurel, and pine respectively. But they were only a springboard to the true finale, the Games of Zeus at Olympia. The crème de la crème would step forward from around the Greek world to face off in the Peloponnesus; no matter how many lesser victories an athlete had racked up, the Olympic Games were the ultimate challenge. And although the top prize was theoretically just an olive wreath, it brought many earthly rewards. Every city in Greece promised generous cash prizes to an athlete who brought home an Olympic crown; fringe benefits might include triumphant parades, lifetime seats at the amphitheater, generous pensions, civic positions, free meals—not to mention the undying respect of one's peers.

We can guess the incomes of these top Greek athletes from their memorials, where they crowed about their triumphs. Typical was a certain Flavius Metrobius, who won the long-distance footrace at Olympia in A.D. 85: He claimed 140 other victories, the bulk of them in prize games. A century later, the wrestler M. Aurelius Hermagoras managed 156 victories—29 in Sacred Games, 127 in prize games, and one Olympia wreath, in A.D. 177. Back in the fifth century B.C., the unbeatable Theagenes of Thasos was believed to have harvested no less than 1,400 prizes. The lifestyles of these athletes would have been luxurious—from the accumulation of cash rewards to the special treatment they received—and as far removed from those of average citizens as NFL players' today.

No wonder the physician Galen wrote an essay, "On Choosing a Profession," complaining that talented young men were all going into athletics over law or medicine.

The Elimination Rounds

THE CONTESTANTS GATHERED in the gymnasiums of Elis were thus at the pinnacle of their careers. Many knew one another from other competitions around the Mediterranean, and they would eye any strangers carefully, assessing their physiques and comparing reputations. The stakes at Olympia were cruelly high. Among the throngs of athletes, only a handful of victors could achieve immortality, while the many losers would be humiliated in front of the whole world. There were no prizes for second place at the ancient Games; the shame of defeat drove some men to madness, others to suicide.

Trial matches were the key to the training month in Elis. Although not formal heats, they were admirably efficient in clearing an overcrowded field. They allowed athletes to gauge the competition. It was no disgrace for a contestant to exercise his discretion and admit he was out of his league, especially in the contact sports. Some wrestlers and boxers dropped out after they had sparred once or twice, realizing they were outclassed. The arrival of celebrity athletes could cause mass desertion; some even won wreaths unopposed. A Roman-era wrestler boasted on his memorial that his opponents all withdrew the moment they saw him undress. (Once the Games had begun, however, contestants could no longer honorably withdraw. Only once in the entire history of the Games did an athlete pull out at the last minute: In A.D. 25, an Egyptian-Greek *pankratiast* named Sarapoin actually climbed through his barracks window and fled from Olympia the night before his contest. The disgusted judges fined him for cowardice.)

And so the thirty days of training at Elis proceeded in a rather more tense atmosphere than the usual gymnasium idyll. The Mediterranean summer was gathering force, and on truly scorching days, goatskins were strung up to create a shady canopy. But the real trial for many top athletes was submitting to the ten Olympic judges, who among their other duties personally oversaw the workouts. They were renowned as the most demanding and capricious trainers in ancient Greece, sending athletes to extremes of exertion on a whim and maintaining a ruthless discipline. Among the naked throngs, they were easily identified by their long robes and forked rods, which were both the symbol of office and tools for reprimands. Any violation—a finger in a wrestler's eye, for example, or a graceless discus swing—received a quick lash across the spine or buttocks. The air crackled with the sound of these humiliating blows, and any backchat meant instant disqualification from the Games. It must have been a salutary lesson for the more famous Greek athletes, renowned for their inflated egos.

The athletes at Elis ate at a common mess, at fixed hours of the day—ensuring that there were no secret recipes, magic potions, or doping to enhance their performances. The menu is unknown, but we can assume in this bastion of conservatism that it corresponded to the "traditional" athletic diet as defined by ancient authors: barley cakes and unleavened bread, a moderate amount of red meat, feta cheese eaten "straight from the basket" (after the whey was drained off and the cheese was placed in wooden bowls). Honey cakes and other sweets were minimized; wine intake was moderate, but certainly not forbidden.

Controlling athletes' carnal desires was a more complicated business.

Locker Room Libido

IT IS NO exaggeration to say that sex and athletics were always intertwined in Greece: the worship of the male physique was never purely aesthetic, and gymnasiums invariably boasted a statue of Eros among the artworks. If every exercise hall was a potential pickup venue, festival time at Elis only accelerated the lascivious pace. For the Greeks, it was almost a social duty for adult males to take adolescent boys as lovers: Theirs was a mentor-tutor relationship, beneficial to the youngster and often encouraged by the boy's family. (Intellectuals regarded the bond as finer and purer than heterosexual love, which was fatally muddied by women's erratic emotions and the brute need to procreate.) In ancient literature, the young men of Elis were famous for being particularly handsome. Among the crowds who came to watch the monthlong training sessions, teenagers flirted outrageously with potential champions, turning the three gymnasiums of Elis into palaces of pederasty.

For Olympic contestants, temptation could also be stressful: There was considerable debate about the debilitating effects of sexual release on athletic performance, especially in the hotter months of the year. The austere Pythagoreans argued that an athlete should abstain entirely during intensive training. (Some athletes slept with flattened leaden plates over their loins, hoping that the chill and weight of the metal would dampen their nocturnal desires. A certain Cleitomachus, according to the author Aelian, also "turned away when he saw dogs in the act of mating, and walked out of any dinner party if he heard licentious and lewd conversation.") But this was only one school of thought, and judging from the sweaty-palmed literary evidence, not a very popular one. For many athletes at Elis, it would be a busy summer. As the poet Theognis of Megara wrote: "Happy is the lover who after spending time in the Gymnasium goes home to sleep all day long with a beautiful young man." Others raved about the erotic allure of athletic sweat; even beaten-up young boxers could be attractive:

> When Mencharmus, Anticles' son, won the boxing match . . .
> Thrice I kissed him all red with much blood,
> But the blood was sweeter to me than myrrh.

An indication of the hothouse atmosphere is provided in one of Plato's dialogues. Here, Socrates meets a group of teenagers who are languidly posing inside the wrestling school. "Oh, we're just passing the time," one of them explains coquettishly. "We and many other beautiful boys." His interest piqued, Socrates corners a particularly handsome pair, although his seduction technique may not go down in literary history.

"So, son of Demophon"—he smiles—"who is older, you or Lysis?"

"We argue about that," the young man replies. (There were, of course, no birth certificates in ancient Greece, and people often had only vague ideas of their age.)

"Do you also argue about which one of you is the more noble?"

"We certainly do."

"And who is the best-looking?"

The pair of teenagers start giggling—Socrates has broken the ice.

Because of the restrictions on women, heterosexual flirting was more limited—but it did go on in Sparta, where young girls stripped for the same training and tests of strength as the boys. Greek literature is an anthology of paeans to the firm breasts and muscular thighs of these healthy Spartan maidens—one modern American historian, writing with a shaky hand, has compared their mythic allure with today's "California girls"—inciting a form of sex tourism. The love-starved Roman poet Propertius went into paroxysms of desire when he visited Sparta, and openly confessed his aim to leer at naked women. But the poet only wanted to watch; a Roman senator named Palfurius Sura went one step further and wrestled a naked Spartan girl in the ring.

The Long March

TWO DAYS BEFORE the Games, those athletes still standing were called before the judges and addressed in pompous tones:

> If you have exercised yourselves in a manner worthy of the Games—
> If you have been guilty of no slothful or ignoble act—
> May you proceed to Olympia with courage.
> But those of you who have not so practiced:
> Go wherever else you please.

This did not mean the athletes could take a breather. Olympia was forty miles away—and contestants had to walk there in a formal procession, under the blazing sun.

As it left Elis, the column had the air of a traveling circus. It was headed by officials in their purple robes and flower garlands. Athletes followed in their finest white tunics and sandals, flanked by their trainers and family members. Then came the chariots and racehorses; sacrificial animals, including one hundred oxen, brought up the rear. Tagging along were the audience members who had decided to get a head start by catching the pre-Games bouts.

While the Sacred Way to Olympia was one of the better roads in classical Greece, the two-day marathon must have tested athletes' stamina levels. The company paused halfway at the fountain of Pieria to sacrifice a pig—the liver was examined to discern the auspices for the Games—and then camped the night at the riverside village of Letrini.

But few felt weary as they finally entered the verdant valley of the Alpheus and glimpsed the shrine of Olympia. The late-afternoon sun was sparkling from the roof of Zeus's temple, lighting up the marble colonnades and bronze statues of champions. But the truly impressive sight, beyond the spectacle of the sanctuary, must have been the crowd itself.

Spilling across the green countryside in every direction, clustered under canvas tents and cheering them on from the side of the road, were the "endless mass of people" that Lucian had complained about—worshipers of the true Greek religion, sport.

V

Trials of the Ancient Sports Fan

There was a man who thought the journey to Olympia would be too much for him, and Socrates said: "What are you afraid of? Don't you walk around all day in Athens? Don't you walk home to have lunch? And again for dinner? And again to sleep? Don't you see that if you string together all the walking you do in five or six days anyway you could easily cover the distance from Athens to Olympia (210 miles)?"

—XENOPHON, *Memorabilia*

ANCIENT GREEK SPECTATORS could never be accused of being couch potatoes: they had to be in good shape just to get to Olympia. Country roads in the classical era were notoriously bad—there was no central Greek government, and rival cities had no incentive to maintain them—so most travelers went on foot, picking their way over rocky trails that snaked through the mountains and ravines. Socrates was underestimating how long the 210-mile journey might take from Athens: Many would have allowed two weeks to reach the sanctuary, including rest days and stopovers. It was generally regarded as a chore, but the journey did have its compensations, and was itself part of the Olympic Games package. Travelers passed through a traditional rural world, dotted with temples full of sacred relics, encountering vignettes of eerie piety. Olympia was where the aura of divinity was most tangible on earth, Pausanias wrote, and the closer travelers got to their goal, the more the air seemed to glow with a sense of pagan wonder.

Today the road from Athens to Olympia, driven by multitudes of rental cars, follows almost exactly the same route as it did 2,500 years ago—although at times it takes a serious leap of imagination to succeed in recapturing the dreamlike, ancient atmosphere. The initial escape from the Greek capital is smothered under a six-lane highway and encrusted in billboards. But after a few miles, the rural foundation of Greece reasserts itself—and we can at least begin to see some of the same majestic mountain views that groups of rank-and-file Greek spectators once saw as they were trudging toward the Olympic Games around 150 B.C.

Pilgrims of Sport

FANS TRAVELING FROM Athens would have left the city through the southern Dipylon Gate, kissed their fingertips in homage as they passed the last shrines, and set off past Kerameikos cemetery, against whose solemn funerary sculptures prostitutes plied their trade at night. From here, they could take one last glance back at the Acropolis, crowned by the Parthenon and a giant bronze statue of the goddess Athena. Athens was the largest and richest city in mainland Greece, and was universally regarded as the most artistically graceful in the entire Mediterranean world. Athenians themselves were the Parisians of antiquity—vain, verbose, divisive, energetic, cerebral, brilliant, contradictory, and, to non-Athenians, unbearable. Deeply superstitious despite their worship of Reason, they would have made careful sacrifices for a safe journey the day before.

We can picture a group as the highway cuts through the olive fields—perhaps a dozen friends and family walking together for company. The male travelers would all be wearing linen chitons,

A Greek traveler on the road, wearing his cloak and wide-brimmed hat. (From the interior of a Greek drinking cup, c. 500 B.C.)

the loose, sleeveless tunic that was the regulation Greek mufti, made from two squares of white cloth loosely draped over the body, leaving one shoulder exposed. These tunics were usually worn to below the knee, but during travel they were hitched up by a belt to make walking easier. They also wore leather sandals tied up the calves and wide-brimmed hats called *petasoi*. (On vase paintings, these look oddly like sombreros in Sergio Leone movies. Despite their practical value—during storms, travelers could tighten a strap and pull the sides down over their ears— the hats were only worn while traveling, since it was believed that keeping moisture from the hair turned it gray.) There would have been only one or two women in the group: apart from this being an arduous journey, married women had to camp outside the grounds of Olympia, and in conservative Athens, unmarried women and girls would have had trouble getting their fathers' permission to attend the Games (other Greek cities were less restrictive). These intrepid women wore brightly colored ankle-length tunics, with fine hats over hair adorned with ribbons. Some wore brooches and jewelry and carried parasols.

Greek men tended to travel light, with only a pouch slung over their shoulder containing a single change of clothes; a short cape, or *chlamys;* some cooking utensils; and a woolen blanket for bedding. The better-off travelers would have brought a servant to carry this, or a donkey with panniers for provisions. Wealthy women brought more luggage, with cosmetics boxes and gowns, which exasperated misogynist legislators: The Athens city council actually passed a law to limit women's travel allowance to three changes of clothes, although the rule was impossible to enforce. (The truly rich, as we will see, were a different breed, traveling across Greece in luxury safaris.) As for money, it had to be transported in hard cash. Athenians were lucky: Their currency was the euro of the classical era. Stamped with a goggle-eyed owl, the emblem of the city, the silver coin was accepted all over Greece, while the multitude of other Greek coins would have to be taken to money changers at Olympia, who all charged rapacious commissions.

At least the party didn't have to worry about safety. Thanks to the Olympic Truce, they traveled with a degree of confidence unheard of elsewhere in the Mediterranean. They weren't just spectators going to an overhyped sports meet. They were holy pilgrims, and to interfere with them was an act of sacrilege against Zeus himself. This sacred cease-fire was honored throughout the Greek world. Wars were stalled, feuds put aside, highwaymen laid low. Even the all-powerful King Philip of Macedon had to apologize when some of his mercenaries shook down an Athenian traveler on the way to the Olympics: Philip compensated the victim for his financial loss and paid a fine to Elis.

Of all the ancient Greek visions transferred to the modern Olympics, this moratorium on conflict remains the most inspiring ideal.

MOST TRAVELERS ON foot could make fifteen miles a day on decent roads. But although the highway started out well paved from Athens—the route marked frequently by shrines to the patron deity of travelers, Hermes, each carved pillar showing the god's face and an erect penis—conditions quickly deteriorated. To cross the narrow isthmus connecting the peninsula of the Peloponnesus to the rest of Greece, wayfarers had to shuffle in single file along a dangerous, cliffside trail, braving crumbling ledges and scree. In Greek legends, it was here that a villain named Sciron ordered hapless passersby to wash his feet before giving them a swift kick in the face, sending them plunging down into the turquoise sea. It was still a nerve-racking stretch, where travelers might trip and fall to their deaths, or even be dragged down the cliff by panicking mules.

It was a relief, after a week on the road from Athens, to reach Corinth, gateway to the Peloponnesus. This beguiling rest stop was a welcome reminder of the comforts of civilization—luxurious marble arcades lined with splendid drinking shops and a temple to Aphrodite that was attended by hundreds of proficient sex workers. Streams of road-weary travelers from Thebes, Argos, Thessaly, and Megara converged here for some R and R, and were joined by the first contingents of spectators arriving from across the seas. Straddling the Greek isthmus, Corinth was the crossroads of the eastern Mediterranean. Enterprising locals had even built an engineering marvel called the *diolkus* so that boats could be loaded onto wheeled carts on one coast of the isthmus and dragged by slaves over the mountains to the other, thus cutting out two weeks of storm-wracked sailing around Cape Malea.

These international arrivals came from Greek colonies as far away as Cadiz and the Nile delta. As Plato put it, the Greeks perched around the Mediterranean "like frogs around a pond," and for a few silver coins, traveling spectators could sleep on the decks of the innumerable Greek merchant ships crisscrossing the

seas. The vessels were built for stability rather than speed, glid-
ing close to shore under a single square sail, but an ancient cruise
was not without its pleasures: Servants would prepare dinner in
the galley, and wine would be shared among the passengers to
fuel learned conversation under the stars.

FROM CORINTH, ONE could hop a boat west to Elis, but
most took the ancient highway that wound through the mountains of Arcadia. Today, this is still one of the loveliest roads in
Greece. Often no more than a single lane, it coils around villages
perched on precipices, past quiet waterfalls and over archaic
stone bridges. In shady grottoes, men in peaked caps play
backgammon and sip sweet black coffee outside tavernas where
sides of lamb are roasted over coals; orange trees drop their fruit
across the byways; and the road is occasionally blocked by herds
of goats driven by Orthodox priests in black robes and long
white beards who have emerged momentarily from their isolated
retreats.

For ancient travelers, Arcadia was the folkloric heartland of
Greece, ruled by the god Pan, who played his pipes in secret
caves and furiously masturbated. They passed enchanted springs
where lepers swam to cure themselves, clusters of holy men carried saplings on their backs as part of a chthonic fertility rite,
and crowds of women wailed and tore their faces in mourning for
the hero Achilles, who had been killed at Troy many centuries
before. In the forests were tree stumps roughly carved into statues of the gods, and oaks adorned with the horns of sacrificial animals. Wayfarers could pause at remote temples, where for a
modest fee priests would show them mythological artifacts like
the thighbones of giants (actually dinosaur fossils exposed by
earthquakes), the hides of monstrous Gorgons whose hair had
once writhed with snakes, and personal artifacts once belonging
to the heroes Ulysses and King Agamemnon.

For accommodation in these backwaters, travelers stopped at

The mountain of Arcadia, en route to Olympia.

rural inns called *pandokeia* ("places that take all comers")—dark and fetid little boxes with hard, narrow beds, leaky roofs, and mosquito-filled ceilings that make grisly cameo appearances throughout ancient literature. Even the well-to-do often had no choice but to put up in these grim roadside hovels, whose owners were often associated with disease and ill omens: it was believed that if a sick person dreamed of an innkeeper, he or she would soon die. Female hoteliers were widely regarded as witches, who could turn hapless male travelers into mules or magically string them up to the rafters by their genitals. And the cuisine at these sordid pit stops was even worse than at the cheapest roadside diner today: Rumors circulated of unlucky ancient travelers finding human flesh and knucklebones in their stew.

In a way, the rough conditions of the journey to Olympia were all good preparation for the five days at the festival. When weary travelers finally found themselves gazing upon the green river valley of the Alpheus, they might have caught their breath at the sheer beauty of the sanctuary. They would have made their first tour of the site in a daze, drinking in the illustrious artwork, the sheer color and excitement of the crowd, the Stadium they had heard about all their lives. It must have been a thrilling moment.

So long as one was not too finicky about the conditions.

The Bed-and-Beverage Crisis

FOR ANY NEW arrival, the first order of business was to stake out a place to sleep.

Only official ambassadors sent by each city with gifts for Zeus were coddled at the Games. They had reservations at the luxury on-site inn, the Leonidaion—a sumptuous, two-story complex named after Leonidas of Naxos, the visionary philanthropist who built it in the fourth century B.C. These lucky guests could stretch out in one of the twenty suites on each floor—the roomiest were on the corners, thirty-five feet square—all with views of a central courtyard garden filled with flowers and fountains and surrounded by Doric columns. The inn, which in the off-season could be used by wealthy sightseers, was an oasis of calm in the maelstrom of the festival. Everyone else was out in the fields.

Naturally, the upper crust maintained a cushion of luxury. They arrived at Olympia in sumptuous convoys attended by teams of horses, grooms, and stable boys, while their slaves had already raced ahead to the sanctuary to pitch silk tents with copious awnings that re-created all the comforts of home—even marble tiles and floor mosaics, favorite artwork and cedar dining tables, ivory wash basins and statuettes. These high-society sports fans could dine on plates of beaten gold, drink from crystal goblets, and sleep on down pillows, all the while attended by retinues of chefs, secretaries, and servants. The placement of these aristocratic tents around the site required as much diplomacy as seating arrangements at a banquet, some spots being more prestigious than others. The nouveau riche Greeks from Sicily and Asia Minor were particularly flamboyant. In 388 B.C., the tyrant Dionysius I of Syracuse set himself up in an enormous tent of golden silk, with lavish carpets and a team of professional actors to read his poetry. The extra spending did him little good—he was denounced by orators for his cruelty as a ruler, his poetry was booed by the crowd as doggerel, and his tent was looted by an angry mob.

Despite such spasms of violence, there was an unofficial contest among the rich as to who could erect the most opulent tent at Olympia. Some priests deemed this one-upmanship unsavory. Inscriptions have been found at Delphi, for example, ordering limits on the floor space of spectators' tents and on their furnishings, and similar regulations may have been imposed at Olympia. But by the Roman era, all restrictions were gone. The Greeks would never see anything quite like the fabulous retinue of the emperor Nero, who descended on Olympia in A.D. 67 with one thousand wagons like an occupying general. His prancing horses were shod with silver and bridled with gold; his path was swept clean by outriders gaily clad as Africans; handsome Greek boys with faces painted white were engaged to dance around the emperor's carriages for his diversion. At Nero's festival banquets, guests ate from silver plates studded with diamonds, and drank out of goblets carved from great chunks of lapis lazuli. And the emperor certainly made himself at home, picking out which of Olympia's statues he fancied to take back to Rome as souvenirs.

For less exalted spectators, there were various budget options. Early arrivals could rent space in one of the makeshift wooden barracks—dirt-floored structures with leaf roofs—set up by the enterprising merchants of Elis. Like modern youth hostels, what these lodgings lacked in comfort, they made up for in conviviality. When Plato chose one for his festival accommodations, he stayed incognito and made fast friends with his new roommates, eating simple meals with them and going to all the contests together. His fellow sports lovers even came to visit him in Athens, where they discovered his true identity. ("They were amazed at having had such a great man amongst them without recognizing him," reports the second-century-A.D. author Aelian. "He had behaved towards them with modesty and simplicity, and had won the confidence of them all without even resorting to philosophical discussions.")

But these basic shelters filled quickly. Option B was to pitch a tent—usually no more than a sheet of canvas strung between two trees—in surrounding farmland. But the majority of sports fans did not bother with even that. The hot summer evenings meant that spending the night al fresco was an extremely pleasant alternative for easygoing Greeks. Bedding was tossed beneath the covered marble promenades of the sanctuary, between statues or under plane trees. After all, who came to the Games to sleep?

Heat and Dust

BEING FLEXIBLE ON accommodations was one convenient trait of the Greek sports fan. Not being too finicky about personal hygiene was another.

The irregular water supply was an ongoing problem in summer. Rain might not have fallen for several months in this corner of southern Greece, making the chalky waters of the river Alpheus undrinkable, while the Cladeus receded to a stagnant trickle. During heat waves, the lack of water could be dangerous. The spreading plane trees of the Sacred Grove gave little protection from the sun, shelters turned into ovens during the day, and there was no shade at all in the sports arenas, where for religious reasons spectators were actually forbidden to wear hats. Not surprisingly, Lucian reports that spectators would collapse in swarms at the Games from heatstroke, and even expire. The elderly philosopher Thales—who once wrote that water was Nature's most precious gift—is said to have died of dehydration, ironically, in the Olympic festival meadow.

The organizers did what they could to ease the drought. Wells were sunk at the site—nine have been excavated by archaeologists, their interiors lined with shell limestone—and local vendors were appointed to bring fresh drinking water on mule-back from a spring two miles up in the valley, but they could not provide for the masses (forty thousand people could fit into the Stadium; historians have estimated that the total crowd, including workers and hangers-on, could easily have reached seventy thousand). As for washing, the athletes and VIPs had decent bathhouses, but everyone else went dirty. Even before the Games began, the air was thick with the scent of body odor. This pungent Olympic atmosphere was not improved by the thousands of cooking fires lit every morning and night, sending clouds of smoke and billowing ash into spectators' eyes.

And what could the enterprising organizers provide in the way of personal facilities for the hordes? Public sanitation in even the richest Greek cities was never a top priority; it was not until the age of Imperial Rome that large-scale sewers were developed (an engineering triumph, claimed one ancient author, perhaps justifiably, on a par with the Pyramids). At Olympia, the pine forests and the dry riverbeds to the south and west became mass latrines, the odors of which would waft intermittently over the proceedings. In the first century A.D., the Romans built the first permanent toilet block for athletes, with seats for fifteen people to perch together at once. (The ancients did not share our modern obsession with privacy; communal bathrooms were ideal places for exchanging gossip.)

Not surprisingly, summer fevers ripped through the crowd—Lucian, no doubt exaggerating the toll, reports that spectators "would die in droves of the epidemics," presumably gastroenteritis and diarrhea. The huge numbers of blackflies can hardly have helped. The Greeks did not realize they transmitted bacteria, but knew they were a maddening pest—which is why, before every Games, Olympic officials sacrificed at the altar of Zeus Apomyios, "the Averter of Flies," to minimize infestations. It seems they had some success. Pliny the Elder reported that after this ritual, the flies began to perish in droves. Aelian says that the swarms voluntarily retired to the opposite bank of the Alpheus River and returned to Olympia only when the festival was over.

It took nine hundred years for the water situation to be resolved at Olympia. Around A.D. 150, an Athenian multimillionaire named Herodes Atticus paid for an aqueduct and a magnificent drinking fountain, shaped like an enormous yawning oyster and shimmering with a half dozen different-colored marbles. Some critics felt the new luxury was making the Greeks soft. According to Lucian, a loudmouthed Cynic named Peregrinus made a speech denouncing Atticus in A.D. 157—"because the spectators of the Olympic Games ought to endure their thirst and—yes, by Zeus!—even die of dehydration if needs be."

Apparently, Peregrinus made his argument while he was drinking from the fountain itself, which began to enrage the crowd. To escape being stoned, he was forced to hide out by the altar of Zeus. At the next Games, Peregrinus made a speech praising Atticus instead.

VI.

Scenes from the Fringe

It was an excellent place to be if you wanted to hear crowds of wretched philosophers heaping abuse on one another—an endless number of historians reading out their imbecilic writings—innumerable poets reciting their drivel to the wild applause of other poets—gaggles of magicians showing their tricks—throngs of fortune-tellers telling fortunes—countless lawyers perverting justice—or armies of peddlers hawking whatever rubbish came to hand. . . .

—DIO THE GOLDEN-TONGUED, C. A.D. 100

ONCE THEY HAD settled in, wide-eyed spectators strolled around Olympia, running into old friends with the Greek greeting of *chaire!* ("rejoice!"), admiring the statues of the celebrity wrestlers of yore, and identifying the living legends in the training fields. The crowd was a marvel in itself—as diverse as the athletes, only extravagantly dressed. There were the macho Spartan men with their shoulder-length hair and vermilion capes; bejeweled Greek Egyptians with their Ethiopian slaves; Cynic philosophers in ragged robes and matted beards, haranguing the throngs from temple steps, starting arguments and even mob brawls. Married women may have been absent from Olympia—

Artist's re-creation of the Sacred Grove of Zeus, Olympia. The temple contains Phidias' famous statue of Zeus; to the right smoulders the god's Great Altar, a cone of ash built up over the centuries.

they were obliged to camp together on the south side of the river Alpheus—but many unmarried girls could move about freely. In fact, Greek fathers often brought their daughters to the Games with the idea of arranging a wedding match, perhaps even with an Olympic champion. Then there were the less morally upright female contingents, the *pornai,* or "buyable women," imported by pimps nicknamed *pornoboskoi,* or "prostitute shepherds."

In the ancient world, religion was inseparable from everyday life, and each sacred festival was paired with its *panegyreis,* or "profane festival." In Olympia, touts had set up their booths to create a sprawling shantytown north of the sanctuary. (Archaeologists believe that it covered the area where the car park and museum stand at Olympia today.) This tent-city was a spectacular fair, an open marketplace for every known commodity, a Coney Island of the senses. Traveling entertainers from around the Aegean added to the festive atmosphere, including acrobats, dancers, sword swallowers, and professional storytellers. ("Give me a copper coin and I'll tell you a golden story" was one popular pitch.) It seemed that everyone in the Greek world wanted to take advantage of the great gathering for cash or self-promotion—sport profiteers were everywhere—but this was more than a sideshow, it was part of the main event. All of life's pleasures could be found at the Olympic Games, and excited audiences hardly knew where to turn first.

Sports Bars on Wheels

THE ASSOCIATION OF spectator sport with heavy drinking has a long pedigree. On most social occasions, the ancient Greeks were disdainful of public drunkenness—the philosophical principle *meden agan,* "All things in moderation," was engraved on temple pediments—but all festivals were times of release, when the prescribed rules of behavior were relaxed. (As one anonymous Greek wit said: "All things in moderation, including moderation.") At the Olympics, the god of the vine, Dionysus, turned the sprawling tent-city into a round-the-clock debauch. And at this supremely body-conscious gathering, surrounded by so many gym-toned physiques, Greek wine aficionados could be encouraged by the teachings of a doctor named Mnesitheus, who argued that binge drinking had positive, purgative effects on health. He helpfully suggested how to avoid vicious hangovers: Don't drink bad wine, don't eat dried fruit or nuts, and don't go to sleep until you have vomited.

For a quick snifter, spectators at the Games probably sought out one of the wooden carts set up by itinerant wine vendors. These were basically mobile taverns, focus points of conviviality where patrons could gather and discuss the athletic results and weigh in on prospects, with the drinking continuing by torchlight after dark. Wine carts were also popular in sophisticated Greek cities, although they were considered somewhat déclassé, haunted by lowlifes and the poor. But at festival time, they were

eminently convenient, and frequented by all but the most snobbish. Sports fans could choose from amphorae of throaty mainland vintages, known as *trikolytos*—which was not a varietal, but
named after the wine's price, three half pints for an obol (a silver
coin, one-sixth of a drachma). One could buy red, white, or *kir-
rhos*, amber, along with fast food—chickpeas with beets, sliced
sausages, salted pork, and fresh figs.

The rituals of ancient Greek boozing have been cataloged by
the historian James Davidson in his book *Courtesans and Fishcakes*.
A good barman poured his wine from freshly opened clay amphorae, and provided clean springwater for his customer to mix
with each cup. Undiluted ancient wine was potent—some 15 to
16 percent alcohol, compared with today's average of 12.5 percent—and powerfully aromatic, thanks to floating vine debris
and grape seeds, which had to be carefully sieved before drinking.
For the ancients, the usual mix in every cup was two-fifths wine
to three-fifths water; only inebriates drank their wine straight.
Any modern traveler to Greece would recognize the distinctive
resinated tang of ancient wine, which came from the pitch used
to seal the amphorae. (Today in Greece, pine needles are deliber-
ately placed in the wine during maturation, giving retsina its
sharp nose.) The more upmarket Greek wine carts probably provided gimmick drinking vessels—examples have been found by
archaeologists in Athens with names like Joy, Release, or Stop
the Hangover. Some mugs were even painted with erotic scenes,
which would be revealed only when the wine was finished.

Anyone looking for a more solid meal to go with their wine
trawled the caterers' booths. Food at Olympia had to be transported from far afield and be able to survive the summer heat.
There was plenty of the spectators' favorite staple, bread—the
Greeks had seventy-nine types, with different names for each—
and basics like feta cheese, olives, honey cakes, eggs, and nuts.
Local hunters arrived from the forests with freshly caught hares,
boars, stags, and gazelles. Salted fish called *tarichos*, cheap and
portable, was no doubt available, as well as smoked anchovies. If

the critics are to be believed, these private contractors often charged rapacious prices for dubious goods—ancient authors refer to ground dog meat ending up in their sausages. Some Greek festivals tried to ban haggling—Plato wrote that in an ideal republic all prices would be fixed—but at Olympia, the teams of market inspectors appointed by the Elian organizers monitored quality and prices.

Setting up trestle tables around the bars of the tent-city were myriad other entrepreneurs and traveling vendors. Whether one was seeking gifts for potential lovers or souvenir knickknacks for the family back home, the shopping opportunities at Olympia were endless. Peddlers laid out chintzy keepsakes—replicas of famous statues from the sanctuary, glass vials engraved with temple outlines, tiny metal chariots. Others sold curios that had nothing to do with sports—sharks' teeth, petrified wood, ivory flutes in cheetah-skin cases. Spartan merchants paraded their attack dogs, as vicious as pit bulls; there were few sales, as nobody knew how to handle the unpredictable beasts. Astrologers and numerologists plied their trade alongside magic vendors from Thessaly who offered love philters made from horse's sweat and minced lizard's flesh.

In fact, everything in the known world could be found at the Olympic fringe, and bought.

Plato's Retreat

THE SEX MARKET was another integral part of any ancient Greek festival. Promiscuity was encouraged by (male) moralists during religious celebrations, on the vague theory that it would strengthen monogamy during the rest of the year. Teams of prostitutes migrated from sporting event to sporting event around Greece, and may well have been familiar to fans. But in this weird sex-trade circuit, the Olympics reigned supreme. It was said a girl could make as much in five days as she would in a year at home. Merchant ships arriving from Asia Minor and Egypt every four years carried cargoes of women instead of wine.

For those on a budget, there were the *pornai*—usually slaves and most famously from Corinth, where prostitutes maintained a sacred bond with the goddess Aphrodite. Tents were turned into makeshift brothels, nicknamed *kineteria*—literally, "fuck factories"—where the girls could be inspected in translucent tunics as they stood in semicircular ranks, singing softly. One customer noted approvingly: "You can choose from these ladies according to your taste: thin, fat, round, tall, short, young, old, middle-aged or past it. . . . They positively pull you inside, calling the old men 'Little Daddies' and the younger ones 'Little Brothers.' " Hawkers would stand outside: "One obol's the fee; pop right in! No coyness here, no nonsense, no running away, but without delay, the one you want, whichever way you want her. You come out; you tell her where to go; to you, she's nothing."

Boys looking for their first carnal experience in Olympia could consult sex manuals available throughout Greece. Ancient authors regularly mention the most popular of these, by Philaenis of Samos—the *Kama Sutra* of antiquity—but it has not survived. From fragments, we know that it included lists of positions, and that prostitutes charged different rates for each. The cheapest was *kubda,* "bent over," but sports fans at Olympia might have opted for the more energetic and expensive *keles,* or "racehorse," with the woman on top. There are references to another position, which keen historians have translated as "the lion on the cheese grater"; its details have been regrettably lost.

But for the fashionable Greek male, the objects of sexual fantasy were the hetaeras, or courtesans—high-class escort girls. Like Japanese geisha, they were accomplished musicians, light-footed dancers, and versatile conversationalists. As one Greek orator said, common prostitutes might attend to the day-to-day needs of the body, wives were needed for producing heirs, but hetaeras were for true pleasure. They were essential elements at victory banquets, able to act at being seduced by the patrons in exchange for valuable gifts. "Ah yes, the firmness of her body," raved one ancient enthusiast. "The color of her skin, the sweetness of her breath, ye gods! You have to struggle a bit, get slapped and punched by gentle hands. But it's a great pleasure—by Zeus, the greatest."

Married Greek women may have been cloistered away in camps on the south bank of the Alpheus; unmarried women were under the vigilance of their families; but hetaeras—their hair dyed blond, fashionable even then; adorned with gay ribbons, with a jewel in the middle of the forehead; their eyelids shaded with kohl; complexions blanched with white lead—moved with ease through Olympia's best society. They could be spotted swapping witticisms with famous artists, reducing statesmen and philosophers to panting, lovesick wrecks. Students squandered their inheritances on the most beautiful, seeking a broader education than that offered by their tutors at the universities of Athens: As the second-century-A.D. satirist Alciphron relates it, one hetaera recommended a jug of good wine for breakfast, "then we will discourse one to another on the purpose of life—which is pleasure—and you will find that I am philosopher enough to convince you."

Working at Olympia had its difficulties for hetaeras. The heat could wreak havoc with ancient cosmetics, as a character playing that role in one Athenian comedy notes: "If you go out in summer, two streaks of black run from your eyes; perspiration makes a red furrow from your cheeks to your neck; and when your hair touches your face, it's blanched by the white lead." But festival time was when trade was booming. The most famous, high-fee hetaeras, called *megalomisthoi,* might earn enough at the Olympics to purchase a decent villa. The canniest even utilized sports festivals for spreading a little positive PR, much as modern celebrities might take advantage of the Oscars. The lovely Phryne, for example, kept her statuesque figure well covered until the gathering at the Corinth games, when "in full sight of a crowd that had gathered from all over Greece," she removed

A flute girl entertains diners at a festive banquet. (From the interior of a Greek drinking cup, c. 475 B.C., attributed to an artist known as the "Foundry Painter.")

her cloak, let her hair loose, and, clad only in her diaphanous tunic, stepped into the sea. The scene became so notorious that the painter Apelles used her to model Aphrodite rising from the waves. Male hangers-on were just as effervescent and manipulative as the women; stories abound of men becoming addicted to their boyish charms, promising them thoroughbred horses and packs of hunting dogs in exchange for their favors.

THE DIVERSIONS OF the fringe seemed limitless—but even the most distracted member of the crowd rushed forward to get a glimpse of the procession bringing the hundreds of athletes, judges, and notables from Elis late in the afternoon before the festival was to officially start. At last, the months of planning were reaching fruition: The Greek world had come together in the sanctuary of Zeus, beneath the waxing moon.

VII

Let the Games Begin

What is a man but a short-lived creature? He is but the dream of a shadow.
But when a ray of sunshine comes as a gift from the gods—
A brilliant light settles on mortals, and a gentle life.
—PINDAR, *Pythian Ode Number 8,* FIFTH CENTURY B.C.

JUST HOW THEATRICAL were the ancient opening ceremonies on the morning of day one? It's hard not to let our imaginations run riot, blurring Hollywood movies and the pseudoclassical kitsch of our own lavish Olympics rituals. The torch relay, for example, is so ingrained in the modern choreography that most people today assume it was a revival of a pagan tradition—unaware that it was actually concocted for Hitler's Games in Berlin.

The Nazis knew a good propaganda symbol when they saw one. At noon on July 20, 1936, two weeks before the start of the Berlin Games, a Greek "high priestess" and fourteen girls wearing classical robes gathered in the ancient Stadium of Olympia, and used parabolic mirrors to focus the sun's rays on a wand until it burst into flame. As a torch was kindled, a chant went up— "Oh fire, lit in an ancient and sacred place, begin your race"— followed by a ceremony where one of Pindar's Pythian odes was sung to ancient instruments. The so-called Olympic flame was then carried by 3,075 relay runners from Greece, passed from magnesium torch to torch (each one bearing the logo of the German arms manufacturer Krupp), until it finally lit a colossal brazier in the Berlin stadium before the Führer's approving gaze.

In fact, this ceremony never occurred at the ancient Olympics. The modern conception is a mishmash of two quite different pagan traditions that Berlin's masterminds—in particular, Dr. Carl Diem, a leading German scholar who became head of the organizing committee—had brilliantly reworked. Olympia, like all ancient Greek and Roman sanctuaries, *did* have its own eternal flame, which was kept burning for Hestia, goddess of the hearth, in a building called the Prytaneion, or "Magistrate's House." It was used to light all the sacrificial fires at altars throughout the sanctuary. And some other ancient Greek cities did have a *lampadedromia,* or torch race, as part of their local festivals. At Athens, for example, young men wearing nothing but a diadem hung over their foreheads would race in relay teams from the port of Piraeus south of the city to the Acropolis, trying to keep a baton made of flaming reeds from the narthex plant alight until they reached the altar of Prometheus. It must have made a hypnotic sight from the Parthenon, watching the flames weaving like fireflies through the dark streets below. But no torch lighting, relay races, or other pyrotechnic shows ever made their appearance at the ancient Olympic Games.

The "revived" 1936 torch race perfectly fit the Nazi design for the Olympics as a showcase for the New Germany. With its aura of ancient mysticism, the rite linked Nazism to the civilized glories of classical Greece, which the Reich's academics were arguing had been an Aryan wonderland. (They were particularly fond of the macho, warlike Spartans—Hitler was even inexplicably convinced that the peasant soup of Schleswig-Holstein was a descendant of Spartan black broth, a famously austere staple fed to the men in communal messes as they underwent their brutal training.) Hitler took considerable personal interest in the ritual, and pumped funds into its promotion: The Nazi propaganda machine covered the torch relay slavishly, broadcast radio reports from every step of the route, and filled the Games with the iconography of ancient Greek athletics. Afterward, the ceremony became permanently embedded in the popular imagination in part due to Leni Riefenstahl's documentary of the Nazi Games, *Olympia,* which evocatively showed a Greek runner treading the gentle beaches of the Aegean at dusk.

Ironically, considering its repellent origins, the torch race has come to symbolize international brotherhood today, and remains a centerpiece of our own pomp-filled Olympic opening ceremonies. (The most popular part of any Games, they are perennially sold out in advance.) Even more strangely, the mock-pagan ritual is still carried out in Greece. Every four years, local teenage girls gather at the temple of Hera at Olympia dressed in faux-pagan regalia—they even use parabolic mirrors to focus the sun's rays—while runners transmit the flame across the globe, sometimes by airplane, boat, scuba, or camel-back, to each new Olympic stadium. Every summer, the German archaeologists now working at Olympia are peeved to distraction by the hundreds of tourists asking them every day to point out the site of this "ancient" torch-lighting ceremony.

In fact, antiquity's Games began with a pagan ritual that to modern eyes seems far more exotic.

Before the God of Oaths

ON DAY ONE, before dawn, the throng of Olympic athletes woke up and shared a simple breakfast with their fathers and trainers—bread dipped in porridge or wine—then re-formed parade ranks, resuming the same marching order as they had on their progress from Elis the evening before. As the sanctuary was bathed in morning sunlight, the group followed a sacred procession path through Olympia, accompanied by festive music and the cheers of spectators on either side, toward the Bouleuterion,

A torch runner from Leni Riefenstahl's Olympia, *the 1938 film of the Nazi Olympics that helped embed the rite in the popular imagination.*

or council house—Olympics HQ, where the ten *Hellanodikai,* or judges, were now staying. In small groups, the athletes were then invited into the building for a melodramatic swearing-in ceremony.

Inside the dark, torch-lit central chamber, the rite was impeccably staged. Contestants found themselves face-to-face with the ring of solemn judges beneath a towering statue of Zeus Horkios, the God of Oaths—a fierce bronze figure wielding silver-plated thunderbolts in each hand. This was the image at Olympia, wrote Pausanias, "most likely to strike terror into the hearts of the wicked." Laid out at the god's feet were thick steaks cut from a freshly sacrificed boar—their juices dripping to the floor—and a stone tablet, which bore an inscription warning perjurers that they would be smitten to ashes for their wrong-doing. It must have been an unforgettable moment for any competitor when he was invited to step up to the stand before Zeus. There, the athletes—along with their trainers, fathers, and brothers—swore that they would use no foul play to secure victory, and that they had trained for the required ten months beforehand in the manner prescribed by the festival organizers. After all the athletes had made their vows, the judges themselves took the stand and swore they would give their decisions honestly and not reveal anything they had learned in confidence about a competitor.

One unspoken purpose of this oath was to ban magic. Long before steroids, an athlete might enhance his performance with "victory charms" or enchanted potions. The more vindictive might direct black magic toward opponents. Curses would be engraved on thin sheets of lead, rolled up, and buried in cemeteries or tossed into wells, where the dead could carry them to Hades. One such "curse tablet," excavated in Athens, is aimed at a runner named Alkidimos: "Do not allow him to get past the starting lines . . . and if he does get past, make him veer off course and disgrace himself"; another spell dooms a wrestler named Petres the Macedonian to be caught "in the dark air of oblivion," where his strength would be sapped. A wrestler named Eutychion receives what appears to be a cheap formula curse: "Let him be deaf, dumb, mindless, harmless and unable to fight against anyone . . ."

But the more prevalent problem in Greek sports was corruption. From the very beginning of each Games, bribery was on everyone's minds. In fact, when the time came for athletes to approach the Stadium through their private entrance, the last thing they saw was a string of statues warning them against temptation to fix the events. The Olympic judges used the fines levied from corruption prosecutions to erect these sixteen bronze statues of Zeus—known as Zanes—which were inscribed with moral poems (reported Pausanias) "to show that you win at Olympia with the speed of your feet and the strength of your body, not with money."

The first bribery scandal at Olympia—at least, the first that came to light—occurred in 388 B.C., when Eubulus of Thessaly paid off three boxers to throw their fights against him. Their fines financed the first six Zanes. Fifty years later, an Athenian named Kallippos paid his opponents to succumb in the pentathlon, and when this was revealed, a huge penalty was levied on Athens itself. The city refused to pay, and even boycotted the Games, until the Delphic oracle threatened to withhold any more prophecies to Athens. This paid for the second six Zanes. It seems that after these cases, corruption became a regular feature at the Games. The pious Pausanias was shocked that anyone would risk the wrath of Zeus, but even a citizen of the host city Elis had "fallen so low" in 12 B.C.—the father of a young athlete had bribed another father to have his son throw a wrestling match.

The situation appears to have become worse under the later Roman Empire. At the less honorable "prize games" elsewhere in Greece and Asia Minor, where huge sums of money were at stake, victories could be bartered like sacks of grain. According to Philostratus, trainers even turned loan shark, lending money to their own athletes for bribes, and charging hefty rates of interest against the value of the future prize. The low point came at the prestigious games in Corinth: A boxer who had promised three thousand drachmas to an opponent to throw the fight refused to pay. For the first time, the defeated athlete took the matter to official arbitration, and brazenly swore before the altar of Poseidon that he had been promised money to lose.

By comparison, the Olympic Games—the Games of Zeus—were paragons of virtue.

The Divine Sideshow

HAVING COMPLETED THEIR oaths, the athletes had the afternoon off to wander the sanctuary of Olympia. For many, standing in the holiest locale in the pagan world was a humbling moment. Despite the impiety of a few corrupt individuals, the vast majority of Greeks accepted that no man could win an olive wreath in the upcoming Games without the favor of the gods. It did not matter how naturally talented he was or how rigorously he trained; an athlete needed the deities to look benignly upon his efforts. The afternoon of day one was the ideal time to make a sacrifice at one of Olympia's seventy-odd altars, and with the assistance of the sanctuary officials they gathered before the shrines of their chosen gods. They had plenty of choice in the Greek pantheon. There were altars to Zeus, Hercules, and the hero Pelops; Hermes, patron of runners; Poseidon, god of horses; Nike, the goddess of Victory; and a spate of lesser deities, including Opportunity, who was personified as a wing-footed boy hurrying with a pair of scales. The athletes left symbolic offerings—tiny statuettes of chariots or runners, ceremonial discuses, and silver tripods. Wealthier contestants sacrificed a goat, lamb, or pig. After the ritual slaughter, soothsayers would inspect the livers for omens, which would no doubt provide insider information for those spectators interested in placing bets.

For their part, spectators could wander the site enjoying a relaxed, carnival atmosphere. The most popular diversion on the afternoon of day one was the contest for heralds and trumpeters, to choose a team to announce the victors. It took place in the lavishly decorated Echo Colonnade, which was known for its unusual acoustics: Every noise would be echoed seven times, so horn blasts and voices rang up and down the marble floors. The most successful herald in Olympic history was Herodoros of Megara, who won the trumpet contest in ten successive festivals from 328 B.C. Herodoros' lungs were put to good use: In between Olympiads, he famously helped his home city win a war against Argos by blowing on two trumpets simultaneously in battle.

Other spectators went to watch the athletes at their final pre-Games exercises. This was the perfect opportunity to see celebrities up close. Greek muscle men in particular were not shy with their fans, and took the opportunity to entertain the adoring crowds with vaudevillian stunts. At the Olympics of 520 B.C., the famous Milo of Croton came dressed as Hercules with a lion's skin and club. He carried a young bull around the Stadium on his shoulders, then afterward devoured it single-handedly for dinner. Milo's party tricks included challenging men to budge his little finger, standing on a discus as weaklings tried to push him off, and guzzling ten pints of wine in a single draught. He would also wrap a cord around his forehead and hold his breath until it was snapped by the bulging veins. In later years, hulking poseurs would challenge each other to weight-lifting contests before the Games began. Archaeologists have found a sandstone block at Olympia that was inscribed with the words "Bybon son of Pholos tossed this over his head with one hand" (it weighs 315 pounds/143.5 kilograms, so this may have been an exaggeration). A 900-pound/480-kilogram block was found on the Aegean island of Santorini, with the words "Eumastas, son of Critobulus, lifted me from the ground."

But many Greeks, on that first afternoon, opted for more intellectual entertainment.

The Literary Marathon

OLYMPIA WAS UNIQUE among Greek festivals for not including any cultural competitions. (At Apollo's games in Delphi, for example, there were a number of artistic contests,

including poetry, prose, song, dance, sculpture, and oratory competitions.) But this did not mean the arts were absent from
Olympia. Its forty-thousand-plus spectators included the cream
of Greek high society, so the Games represented a major marketing opportunity. Creative types converged here in droves, producing an offstage artistic frenzy—and the relaxed after-lunch
ambiance of day one guaranteed a large and receptive audience.

The first to fully grasp Olympia's PR potential had been
Herodotus, the revered "Father of History" who around 440 B.C.
wanted to promote his newly written account of the Persian
Wars. Why go on an epic book tour around Greece, Italy, and
Asia Minor, he pondered, when one could get the same exposure
overnight at Olympia? As Lucian recounts it, Herodotus waited
until all the notables had arrived at the festival—this appears
from the sources to have been the afternoon of day one—then,
"behaving less like a spectator than an athletic contestant," he
went inside the crowded Temple of Zeus and began to read his
work aloud. It was a smash hit. The audience was mesmerized. As
Lucian relates, "It was not long until he was better known than
the Olympic victors. There was not a man in Greece who hadn't
heard the name of Herodotus, either because they had been at
Olympia, or were told about him by returning spectators."

A tradition was begun—appearing at Olympia, preferably on
the first day for maximum impact, became the literary "short-cut
to fame." In Herodotus' audience was a young aspiring wordsmith
named Thucydides who, according to legend, was moved to tears,
and would later write his majestic history of the Peloponnesian
Wars (and naturally debut it at Olympia). Other writers soon followed suit. Inspired poets took to the temple steps in snow-white
tunics and sang their works while strumming a lyre with an ivory
pluck. Some were hailed with cries of *Euge!*—"Bravo!" Others
were mocked. Greek audiences were discerning, and were not distracted by displays of wealth. The tyrant Dionysius of Sicily had
his verse read by the finest professional actors, but it was so bad
that the crowd looted his tent. When the emperor Nero per-

formed his epic poem about the fall of Troy at the Olympic Games, one wit complained, it provoked "whole *Iliad*s of woe."

Philosophers quickly seized the potential: soon every soapbox orator in Greece was converging to add his voice to the chorus. In an early show of antisports snobbery, Diogenes said that it was his social duty to speak to athletics fans: "Just as a good doctor rushes to help in places full of the sick, so it was necessary for a wise man to go where idiots proliferate." His fellow Cynic philosophers, who reviled all the trappings of civilization, became a fixture at the Games. Antiquity's hippies, they wore their hair unkempt, dressed in rags, mooched meals, and railed against every Greek sacred cow. But the heroes of Greek philosophy also put in appearances, and geniuses like Aristotle even had their statues raised at Olympia alongside those of athletes. The PR potential of the Olympic Games was so established by the first century A.D. that the pagan holy man Apollonius of Tyana even sent his own advance guard to whip up interest. Thousands attended his sermons on wisdom and temperance, but Apollonius resented sharing the limelight with hack writers. Exasperated by the drivel, he cornered one "literary puppy" who intended to recite an epic poem about Zeus. When the youngster read his own poems on gout and deafness, Apollonius sarcastically noted that he should write one on something really interesting, like influenza. He then chewed the youngster out for even attempting to depict Zeus: "You are embarking on a subject that transcends the power of mortals!"

ANCIENT PAINTERS TOO attended the Olympics, to show off new work and burnish their reputations, taking advantage of the opening-day crowds. It seems many were natural showmen. Around 420 B.C., the egomaniacal Zeuxis of Heraclea appeared, wearing a loud checkered tunic with his name embroidered ostentatiously in gilt letters. He presented his best paintings to royal visitors, explaining that they were priceless masterpieces so he could not take money for them. He was joined by dozens of lesser lights who turned the colonnades into impromptu galleries, where aficionados could inspect new works that invariably represented mythological themes or athletics. The great Parrhasius of Ephesus, a Falstaffian figure who sang as he painted, was most famous for "The Runner," an image so realistic that viewers expected sweat to drip from the picture (sadly, it does not survive—nor, indeed, does any Greek easel painting, apart from a scrap of blue found in Delphi). For emerging artists, a visit could pay high dividends. In the fifth century B.C., an Olympic judge liked one young painter's work so much that he gave him his beautiful daughter in marriage. And for spectators, having one's portrait commissioned was a quick souvenir. A papyrus from A.D. 362 shows a portraitist's fee to be one sack of wheat and two amphorae of wine.

The Beefcake Gallery

AMONG THE BODY worshipers of ancient Greece, sculptors had the most kudos. Sport was one of the great motors of Western art, and Olympia was the Greeks' permanent national gallery: Every victor had the right to a life-sized statue placed here, so the fields between temples became an increasingly crowded sea of glistening torsos (they were invariably made of bronze—only the Roman copies that survive today were marble). Prattling tour guides would do the rounds of the Old Masters of the seventh and early sixth century B.C., whose statues were rather stiff and formal. After 500 B.C., thanks to the work of artists like Polykleitus and Lysippus, a suggestion of movement began to bring the inert figures to life, and this eventually led to the illustrious classical achievements of artists like Myron with his "Discus Thrower" around 470 B.C. Almost all of these later sculptures were re-creations of an ideal male form—the Apolline figure made manifest, capturing youthful strength, harmony, good looks, and sublime inner beauty (great artists would devise their own *kanon* regulating the best proportion of limbs for statues). Only after winning three times at Olympia did an athlete have the right to erect a more realistic "portrait statue" of himself, showing his actual face and form.

Some Olympic statues were thought to possess magical properties. The figure of Pulydamas, for example, could supposedly cure fevers (which must have come in handy in Olympia's unhygienic conditions). The statue of Theagenes of Thasos was even more powerful. According to a bizarre account from Pausanias, it had once fallen and crushed a man to death; the victim, a former opponent of the champion, happened to be whipping the image when the accident happened. The statue was actually placed on trial for murder by Elian officials, and sentenced to be thrown into the sea. When the fields around Olympia bore no fruit for several seasons, the Delphic oracle ordered that the statue should be fished up from the sea again, returned to its place, and worshiped as sacred.

AND SO WE can imagine ancient Olympians strolling amongst these frozen figures on that balmy first evening of the Games, reading moonlit inscriptions from centuries past.

> Sostratus, son of Sosistratus. Thou didst glorify
> thy native Sicyon by winning very many
> and very glorious crowns . . .

> Eurhythmus, a Locrian, son of Astycles, was
> thrice victorious at Olympia, and he set up
> this statue for mortals to behold.

> You are looking at the glorious form of
> Charmides, an Elian boxer, in memorial
> to an Olympic victory.

In the coming days, the athletes hoped, they too might achieve immortality.

VIII.

Blood on the Tracks— the Chariot Race

Again comes the shock of axle on axle, of spokes on spokes; no mercy is asked or quarter given; one would think the drivers were pitted in savage war, so furious is their will to win, so ever-present the threat of a gory death.

—STATIUS, *Thebaid*, FIRST CENTURY A.D.

ANCIENT EVENT PLANNERS did not believe in delayed gratification: The Olympic program kicked off on a spectacular high on the morning of day two, with the most eagerly antici-pated of all contests, the four-horse chariot race. This was a dra-matic and lethal affair whose details Hollywood, for once, has not exaggerated. In fact, movie epics like *Ben-Hur* give quite an accurate idea of a chariot race's delirious start, the confusion that would grow with each lap, and, above all, the sudden violence of the accidents. At Olympia, some forty vehicles would crowd the course and bloody crashes were guaranteed; after one particularly intense race, only a single vehicle managed to cross the finishing line. Even in Greek mythology, when the beloved hero Pelops had raced a chariot from Olympia for the hand of a princess, he caused the death of King Oinomaos (more about them later). Now, with its combination of glamour and high risk, the

A chariot is harnessed before the race (from a Greek water jar, c. 520 B.C.).

Olympic chariot race was the Grand Prix of antiquity—and the bareback horse races that filled up the rest of the morning's program were hardly less murderous. By midday, some unlucky riders would be on the way to Hades, while others, blessed by the gods, would be celebrating with garlands in their hair. As if to recognize their fatal gamble, the day's events would conclude with a haunting sacrifice of a black ram beneath the rising full moon, in which a priest poured the animal's warm blood onto the burial mound of Pelops himself.

The excitement began before sunrise. Spectators pressed forward toward a field to the east of the Hippodrome, where the charioteers were preparing in front of a marble colonnade, called the Portico of Agapantus. It must have been a spectacular scene, as colorful and chaotic as a Homeric army readying for war. Racing was traditionally the sport of kings in ancient Greece—one had to be very rich to maintain a stable of stallions—and it was

A Hollywood re-creation of a chariot race in Ben-Hur *(1959).*

still Olympia's most aristocratic event. During the pre-Games period in Elis, weaker teams had been weeded out during practice rounds. Now forty magnificent vehicles were being tethered and yoked, and the pasture was home to a whole cavalry of thoroughbreds with names like Wolf and Breeze, their coats washed and gleaming with oil, kicking up dust in the first golden light. Grooms dashed back and forth on errands; wealthy owners came by for final inspections; the charioteers themselves, in their brilliant white robes, made their last vows to Poseidon, patron deity of horses.

Fans paid attention to every detail, weighing up the chances of each vehicle. There was no formal betting system, but ancient Greeks loved to gamble, and made friendly wagers on the race; true enthusiasts had watched the horses exercising and even sniffed their dung in the pastures, to learn the quality of their fodder. The four horses on each team ran abreast, with the strongest pair placed in the center of the quartet, tethered securely to the chariot's pole; the outer pair, chosen for agility in the turns, were connected by leather straps. All had ornamental reins and bits, and in some cases jewel-encrusted nosebands. True to the chariot races depicted by Cecil B. DeMille, the rigs were fragile shells, made of light wood or wicker for speed. The design had not changed since the time of the Trojan War: They were authentic war chariots, but brightly painted, decorated with leather, sheet bronze, and silver inlay.

The crowd was thick with flamboyant young noblemen greeting one another, along with ambassadors and foreign dignitaries in their most regal outfits. Taking advantage of the potential for business, the most beautiful courtesans made cameo appearances, sparkling with expensive silk and jewelry (fashion and racing were intimately connected long before the Royal Ascot). This was the day at Olympia for extravagant gestures. The charismatic and dashing young Athenian Alcibiades famously entered seven chariots in the race of 416 B.C. He even arranged history's first sports-sponsorship deal, convincing the island of Chios to provision the stables for his twenty-eight horses. It was the celebrity owner of the chariot, not the driver, who received the accolades if he won; like Thoroughbred jockeys today, the charioteers were strictly professionals hired for the event, and only the most generous of noblemen let his driver be remembered in a statue or victory song. However, those few aristocrats who did risk their lives on the track were even more celebrated: In the fifth century B.C., Herodotos of Thebes is praised in one of Pindar's odes for taking the reins himself, while a Spartan named Damonon and his son Enymakratidas together pulled in sixty-eight equestrian victories at eight local festivals. The pair erected a splendid monument to themselves, and would be remembered for centuries.

This system of owners "winning" the chariot races had one progressive side effect: It allowed women to circumvent the ban on their participation in the Olympics. This feminist breakthrough was made by a Spartan princess named Cynisca, who won with her chariots twice, in 396 and 392 B.C. She erected a lavish memorial thanking Zeus for her triumphs; in the centuries that followed, other brash noblewomen followed her example.

Perhaps not surprisingly, given the danger, charioteers were a superstitious bunch. They put charms on their vehicles—a model phallus to ward off vindictive spells, and drawings of concentric circles as protection against the evil eye (a symbol that is found throughout Greece and Turkey today). Chariot races were favorite targets for black magic. Rival owners, jockeys, and gamblers paid witches to place curses on opponents' horses ("Drive them mad, without muscles, without limbs," reads one lead curse tablet excavated by archaeologists, "let them be unable to run or walk or achieve victory, or even leave the starting gates . . ."). Other spells were aimed at the hapless charioteers themselves: "I bind the hands [of drivers] . . . send them blind . . . let them be tossed to the ground, so that they are dragged by their own vehicles throughout the Hippodrome. . . ."

No wonder the charioteers felt vulnerable as the crowds inspected their rigs. As the poet Statius said, "The thrill of courage mixed with dread ran through their fingertips and toes."

The Sacred Turf

HAVING HAD THEIR fill of ogling the chariots, eager spectators elbowed their way into the Hippodrome itself. Modern archaeologists have found no trace of this eponymous horse track—it was washed away by floods during the Middle Ages—but we know that it was located in the flat river plain to the south of the Stadium. The descriptions of ancient sports fans allow us to reconstruct its appearance. Unlike the grandiose urban circuses of the Romans, with their rows of stone seats and enormous obelisks, the Hippodrome at Olympia made the best of its natural setting. The noisy crowds stood on steep grass embankments, with the front rows protected only by flimsy wooden barriers erected around the track. The racecourse itself was six hundred yards long by two hundred wide—three times larger than the Stadium—and defined only by two stone pillars, marking the turns at each end. All around the arena were altars, plaques, statues, and offerings, including hundreds of tiny chariots and wheels, commemorating past victories and disasters.

The purple-robed judges solemnly took their seats in a ceremonial box, located by the finishing line, but spectators preferred better views of the accidents, and clustered most heavily near the turning posts. These two stone pillars reminded the crowd that the turf before them was laden with myth: Mounted on both were bronze statues of the beautiful princess Hippodameia crowning the victorious Pelops. Pelops was actually the hero most beloved by athletes at Olympia, and was the particular patron of charioteers. He was probably a real historical figure whose exploits were enhanced over the centuries by Greek legend. Drivers and spectators alike enjoyed recounting the saga of his success.

According to mythology, King Oinomaos of Elis had devised a deadly courtship ritual for the hand of his daughter: He allowed prospective suitors to drive off with her in a chariot from Olympia, and the king would pursue them in his royal vehicle. It was literally a race to the death: If the suitor was faster, he could marry the princess; if he was caught, he would be speared by the king. None had escaped. A dozen men's heads were nailed to the palace gates when the handsome wanderer Pelops arrived to take up the challenge (the date, historians guess, was around 1280 B.C.). But Pelops decided to leave nothing to chance: He bribed the royal charioteer, Myrtilos, to loosen the king's axle pins. The next day, when Oinomaos raced off in pursuit of Pelops, the wheels of his chariot flew off, the king was killed, and bolts of lightning rained down from heaven to incinerate his palace. Pelops married the lovely Hippodameia and assumed the kingship of Elis. But rather than thanking the treacherous Myrtilos for his victory, Pelops flung him from a cliff.

It might seem a little disconcerting that this so-called hero had won his victory by bribery and chicanery. But Greeks took pleasure in the cunning of Pelops, reveled in his character, and forgave his methods. The tale was beloved in the same way as anecdotes about our own flawed sports heroes such as Babe Ruth and John McEnroe.

AS TRUMPETS SOUNDED, the charioteers entered the Hippodrome in a splendid single-file procession, the horses high-stepping around the track. The riders held the reins in the left hand; in the right, they carried whips or goads—long sticks with bells or jingles on the end. One by one they would approach the judges in the company of the chariot owner. Heralds proclaimed the name of each competitor, his father, and his city, then asked if anyone in the crowd had any charge to bring against him. At the end of this, the head judge gave a long-winded address to the assembled group. Finally, each charioteer drew a lot from a ceremonial urn and cantered off to take his position in the starting gate—which happened to be one of the strangest contraptions in sporting history.

Called the *aphesis,* Olympia's starting gate was a typically ingenious Greek solution to a perennial racing problem. At other top-ranking tracks like Delphi and Corinth, chariots simply started in a line at the sound of a trumpet, which meant that vehicles at the end had to run farther to reach the first turning post—a critical disadvantage in any race. To promote fairness, an Athenian inventor named Kleotas designed a gate in the shape of an enormous triangle. It protruded onto the turf like a ship's prow, with booths for each chariot and an elaborate crank system that opened the forty gates in reverse order, letting the last charioteers burst onto the track first. This clockwork creation made practical use of the Greek advances in geometry: By staggering the start, every chariot had a more or less equal chance of reaching the first post, eliminating the insider's advantage. Judging from ancient descriptions, the *aphesis* was a strange and wonderful sight, decorated with a bronze dolphin and a gleaming eagle that were both part of the working mechanism. Naturally, it took time for charioteers to negotiate their way into their designated gates, adding to the excitement in the crowd. Old men, former drivers, boasted of their own experiences; others recalled the advice of King Nestor to his son in Homer's *Iliad*—that it is not always the fastest horses that win a race; the skill of the charioteer is paramount:

> *One type of driver trusts his horses and car*
> *And swerves mindlessly this way and that,*
> *All over the course, without reining his horses.*
> *But a man who knows how to win with lesser horses*
> *Keeps his eye on the post and cuts the turn close,*
> *And from the start keeps tension on the reins*
> *With a firm hand as he watches the leader.*

Once the starting mechanism was set—the horses champing at their bits, wrote the poet Statius in another vivid description of a Greek chariot race, "their eyes darting flame, they smoke and pant in stifled rage"—the chief judge signaled by dropping a handkerchief. An official immediately pulled a lever, and the great machinery cranked into motion like a vast toy clock. The bronze dolphin began to drop, the eagle rose, and, accompanied by a trumpet blast, the gates began to open.

It must have been a breathtaking sight, as two chariots at a time pounded out of the gates, until all forty were on their way. Greek poets competed with one another to come up with fresh metaphors for their speed, saying the vehicles shot forth "like javelins," "swift as Harpies," "fast as a torrential river," roaring "like a whirlwind," like lightning or shooting stars. Sophocles gives us a more concrete glimpse of the scene: "The clatter of the chariots filled the whole arena, and the dust flew up to heaven. They sped along in a dense mass, with every driver cracking the whip to break out of the pack, trying to leave behind the whirling axles and snorting steeds, and each man saw his wheels being splattered with foam, and felt the hot breath of rival horses on his back."

The 180-degree angle of the turn posed a deadly test of skill. The left hub had to pass the post without scraping it. Drivers who misjudged were tossed over the rail, entangled in the reins, while their horses ran wild over the course, to the screams of the crowd. The unlucky would go under the hooves of the following chariot, causing multiple pile-ups.

And those who made it safely could not relax for long—there were twenty-three turns in each race.

THE CHARIOTS TOOK only fifteen minutes to cover the twelve double laps—about six miles—but the time seemed like an eternity, with every turn producing new catastrophes and triumphs of skill. The charioteers were agonized by stress, bouncing over rutted ground that they had to scan desperately for debris. The roar of the crowd was deafening. "Who can describe your shouts," asked the orator Dio the Golden-Tongued, "the commotion and the agony, the bodily contortions and groans, the awful curses you utter? The horses won't go any slower if you behave with decorum." Down on the track, the very air, wrote Statius, "hissed with the sound of the oft-plied lash."

Again, divine intervention was crucial, for better or worse. At Olympia, drivers feared the eastern turning post, because here they had to pass an altar known as Taraxippus, the "horse terrorizer"—a small stone shrine that was believed to strike mad panic into horses and cause innumerable accidents. Learned scholars like Pausanias debated the magical causes of the phenomenon. (Was the spot haunted by a demon or cursed by witchcraft? Was it the grave of the royal charioteer Myrtilos, murdered by Pelops? Or were the bones of King Oinomaos himself buried here, his ghost forever taking revenge for his untimely death?) Modern historians have observed that the altar was located precisely where the early-morning sun blasted into the eyes of charioteers and horses as they sped along the southern track, accentuating their confusion and cranking up the danger.

Teams of Olympic attendants were poised to drag mangled chariots out of the oncoming traffic and calm maddened horses. Sophocles describes one accident: "As the crowd saw the driver somersault, there rose a wail of pity for the youth, as he was bounced onto the ground, then flung head over heels into the sky. When his companions caught the runaway team and freed the blood-stained corpse from his rig, he was disfigured and marred past the recognition of his best friend." There are no accounts of incidents when chariots careened into the audience, but it would have been a statistical certainty.

As Homer observed:

> The chariots sometimes rolled, sometimes hurtled
> Over the ground, and the drivers stood in them
> With their hearts pounding for victory, calling
> To their horses, who flew along in the dust.

The crowd was at a fever pitch as the chariots reached the last lap, announced by another trumpet blast. Spectators shrieked, swore, wept, tore their hair, and hid their faces, their cries drowning out the thundering hooves. As the dust settled, the racetrack resembled the aftermath of a battle more than a sporting event. The winning charioteer leapt from his rig, his snow-white tunic now filthy, his face encrusted with dust, and approached the judges—where he was joined by the owner, still clean and perfumed, with fragrant hair. The owner would later receive the wreath at the awards ceremony, but for now the driver shared the adulation of the crowd. Both men would have the victory ribbons wrapped around their foreheads and arms, while the spectators roared their approval and showered them with flowers and olive twigs.

ALTHOUGH THE IMPARTIALITY of the Elian judges was legendary throughout Greece, there were occasional arguments about split decisions, errors, and favoritism, especially in the equestrian events. Not only could fellow Elians enter horses—they were famous for their stud farms—but the judges *themselves* would enter. This peculiar situation erupted in a scandal in 372 B.C., when a judge named Troilus won two of the three chariot races. The subsequent ill will convinced the Elians to ban judges from competing—although Troilus kept his pair of olive wreaths, and erected a statue in his own honor.

But the low point in Olympic judging came in the Roman era, when the emperor Nero decided to compete in the Games of A.D. 67 and debut in the chariot race. The judges, after accepting monstrous bribes of 250,000 drachmas per head, bowed to the emperor's every wish. Nero arrived at the racetrack with an unwieldy ten-horse chariot. He was thrown from his rig and failed to finish the course, but the judges magnanimously declared him the victor anyway. At the victory banquet, the emperor declared: "The Greeks alone know how to appreciate me." Olympia, however, did regain its self-respect. The next year, Nero was murdered in Rome. His name was struck from the victors' list, and the judges were ordered to pay back their bribes.

The Pentathlon

An athlete with fast legs and a long stride makes a good runner. One who can grab and grapple makes a good wrestler. . . . One who excels in both boxing and wrestling makes a good pankratiast. But he who excels in everything is fit for the pentathlon.
— ARISTOTLE, *Rhetoric*, C. 330 B.C.

AROUND NOON ON day two, a herald blasted a trumpet in the Sacred Grove, alerting the crowds to take their places on the grassy banks of the Stadium. A bulletin board confirmed that the hour had arrived for the first track-and-field event at Olympia: the pentathlon.

For audience members, it was an uncomfortable squeeze. The Stadium was only about a third of the Hippodrome's length, so despite vigorous attempts to cater to the throngs—the southern bank had been artificially raised twenty feet by landfill, and the sides of the running track made slightly convex to provide better views—it was standing-room only. Epictetus writes vividly of the crowds, pushing and shoving their way forward, all beneath a midday sky that was like a white bowl of heat. But wilting spectators were buoyed by the heady aura of legend that filled the arena—legend that could fire the least poetic imagination.

On this very spot, it was said, the gods themselves had once competed at athletics (Apollo had beaten Hermes in a running race, and Ares, god of war, at boxing). The running track, now freshly sprinkled with white sand, had originally been paced out by Hercules. And upon the Hill of Kronos, which rose to the Stadium's north, Zeus had wrestled his Titan father for control of the world. The fact that the grassy arena had been remodeled twice in Olympia's long history did not bother spectators in the least; this was still the living site of Greek myth.

The athletes, meanwhile, were waiting impatiently for their summons in a private disrobing hall. This refuge from the crowds, only recently found by archaeologists at Olympia, was designed around 330 B.C. so the competitors could prepare, oil themselves, and relax before their events. It was a hundred-yard-long corridor along the west end of the Stadium, lined with benches, half open to the sky and half covered by an awning. To make the contestants' entrance into the Stadium as theatrical as possible, a vaulted stone passageway was built from the disrobing hall into the western embankment (Pausanias dubbed it, breathlessly, the Secret Tunnel). It was inside this humid, forty-yard-long corridor lit by flickering torches that the athletes were ushered before the pentathlon, to await being called by name. The tension underground must have been enormous as the competitors made their last vows and amused themselves by engraving graffiti on the stone walls (possibly using the tips of javelins kept there). No messages survive from Olympia's tunnel, but the entrance to Nemea stadium gives an idea of the typical outpourings: Of the dozen legible examples, most athletes just scratched their names—Telestas, Polyxenos, Andreas, Epikrates, and Timostratos—but a love-struck soul wrote, "Akrotatos is beautiful." Another, perhaps Akrotatos himself, responds: "Says who?" Someone else crows, "I win." And the final word from the champions of ancient Greece: "Look up Moschos in Philippi—he's cute."

A trumpet blared, the herald called out a name (the order may have been chosen by lot), and one by one the athletes burst into the brilliant light of the arena to the tumultuous roar of the forty thousand–strong crowd. As they ran forward to the judges, they passed their trainers, who were in their own section of the stands, behind a wooden fence. The coaches were as naked as the athletes—a rule that had been devised in 404 B.C., when a married woman had scandalously slipped into the Games disguised in a trainer's tunic. Once the athletes were introduced—there were usually twenty competitors—the three judges running the pentathlon signaled for the official equipment to be fetched.

The pentathlon's popularity stemmed from the way it showcased the gamut of physical prowess. Here, the all-rounder had his day, working through a sampler of the Greek athletic tradition—discus, javelin, long jump, running, and wrestling. According to ancient scholars, the contest had first been performed by Jason and his Argonauts when, during an island stopover in the quest for the Golden Fleece, Jason came up with the idea of combining the crew's five favorite sports to decide who was the most versatile athlete. The innovation stuck. Learned philosophers like Aristotle, who were opposed to overspecialization in sport, admired the pentathlete above all others for his combination of agility, speed, and strength—as did artists and critics. "The pentathlete should be heavy rather than light, and light rather than heavy," intones the coach-aesthete Philostratus. "He should be tall, well-built, with good posture, not too bulked-up, nor too wiry . . ." He also needed good flexibility, strong hips, and long fingers. Music played in the long jump helped emphasize this proximity to the Greek ideal of physical harmony.

Of the afternoon's five events, three were unique to the pentathlon—discus, javelin, and long jump—and they were given such priority that one historian has said the contest was more of a triathlon. (Sprinting and wrestling as main events were scheduled later in the Games for specialists.) The rules for judging the pentathlon are surprisingly obscure, but it seems most probable that every pentathlete competed in the three core events, and if a single athlete won them all, he was declared victor. If no clear winner emerged, the best athletes entered the running race. Only if there was still no obvious victor did those who had not been eliminated meet in the wrestling, as a tiebreaker.

MYRON'S "DISCUS THROWER" (*discobolos*) may be the most famous of all Greek athletic statues today, reproduced on coffee cups in Greek diners around the world, while replica statuettes grace the mantelpieces of millions of tourists. Anyone can conjure up the image: it is a masterpiece of physical fluidity, capturing the athlete at the back of his swing, every muscle stretched before stepping into the throw. The figure's expression, one modern art critic has discerned, is confident and serene, "not heavy or brutal, but that of a man of blood and refinement, who could write books if he would condescend." But like everything else in the classical Greek world, its familiarity is deceptive. The bronze original of Myron's chef d'oeuvre, cast around 470 B.C., was lost; our only reference to the original is from a trio of marble Roman copies made centuries later. Only one of those is intact (it is in the Museo Nazionale in Rome); of the other pair, in the British Museum and the Vatican, only the torsos remain, and the figures were incorrectly restored using parts from other ancient statues. Their heads were placed facing forward, whereas they should be facing down toward the discus, which helped with momentum.

Following the call for the equipment, three official discuses arrived from the Treasury of the Sicyonians, one of the shrines sponsored by different Greek cities to store valuables. There was no standard size for ancient discuses: competitors used a different set at each venue. Olympia's versions were notoriously heavy, probably made of bronze and inscribed with sacred messages around the rim. We cannot be certain because the three famous

Discus throwers take their stances before the swing. (From two Athenian vases, fifth century B.C.)

competition discuses have been lost. Archaeologists, however, have excavated some twenty other examples throughout Greece, including eight from Olympia itself. Engraved with athletes' names, they may have been temple offerings or practice discuses. The bronze examples weigh between three and nine pounds, compared to two kilograms/4.4 pounds for the men's discus in competition today; they vary in diameter from seven to thirteen inches, and are usually less than an inch thick. (Those made of lead and marble weigh up to 8.5 kilograms/18.75 pounds, but were apparently ceremonial pieces.)

Our ancient athletes threw from the eastern end of the Stadium. The first contestant took his position—within three lines marked out the shape of an open-sided square—and dusted his discus with sand, slipping his fingers around the dented rim to find the point that best suited his grip. The ancient throwing style was considerably more constricted than the modern, and as tightly choreographed as a tango. Taking his stance with his left foot forward, the athlete slowly raised the discus in both hands until it was above his forehead. He swung the discus back in the right hand to the position held by Myron's "Discus Thrower," then with a three-quarter twist of the body stepped forward onto his right foot and let fly—"flinging it with a mighty swirl," says Statius, "springing after it himself." Some dropped the discus in the downswing, provoking groans from the crowd; others

An ancient discus thrower poised to let fly in Leni Riefenstahl's Olympia *(1938).*

"buried it in the clouds," to roars of approval. Olympic attendants marked the landing spot with a peg; then the next athlete stepped up to the line. Each athlete had five throws.

How did this peculiarly stylized sport come about? The word *diskos* originally meant "a thing for throwing," and the first competitions appear to have been various forms of shot put, using large stones and metal lumps. The birth of the flat, circular shape was probably a happy coincidence of tradition and practical experience. In *The Iliad,* Achilles offers a valuable ingot of iron as the prize to the man who can toss it farthest, and we know that these were molded in the sand in the shape of smooth round cakes, curved on one side and flat on the other. As any schoolboy quickly discovers when tossing stones into a pond, this shape can be propelled the farthest, so by the time the pentathlon was introduced to the Olympics in 708 B.C., it had become standard issue.

When the Olympic Games fell into oblivion after antiquity, the art of discus throwing was lost. It was only re-created in the 1880s by outdoor-loving British sport historians at Cambridge and Oxford, and as a result the Greeks enthusiastically included it in the revived Olympics of 1896 in Athens. But the ancient swing, which allows only a three-quarter twist of the body, has been replaced by a free-style swing that allows an athlete to spin his body twice before propelling the discus; the modern version adds significantly more centrifugal force to the toss, allowing lengths of over sixty-five meters/two hundred feet. What lengths were ancient Greeks able to achieve at the Olympics? Unfortunately, the only record that we have was made around 480 B.C., when a famous pentathlete named Phayllos, a military hero in the Persian Wars, tossed the discus ninety-five feet. Modern athletes re-creating the Greek style have achieved tosses of 120 feet, although the weight of the ancient discus is an unknown factor. The only other discus record in ancient literature is even less useful as a comparison. A ghost on the shores of the Hellespont was said to spend his nights tossing a discus "twice as heavy as that of Olympia." This supernatural athlete managed, apparently, one hundred cubits (45.7 meters).

The restricted windup may not have enabled much distance in a throw, but its elegance appealed to the Greeks. It also served another useful purpose: control. While the field allocated to a modern discus thrower is a wide arc allowing up to ninety degrees' leeway, the ancient toss had to stay within the slender rectangle of the Stadium, only ninety feet wide. Needless to say, there were incidents—even the god Apollo accidentally brained the beautiful youth Hyacinthus with a discus that was carried off course by the malicious god of wind. (A flower emerged from his blood, marked with the letters *AI AI,* "Alas, alas.")

But spectators were far more nervous at the next event.

THE OLYMPIC JAVELINS were brought forward. This was the most martial of ancient sports: Greek boys had been raised using it for army training at the gymnasium and for hunting on horseback. The javelins used for athletics were made of lighter wood than military issue; they stood about the height of a man, and were a finger's thickness. Blunt versions were usually used for practice, but at the Olympics, sharp javelins were used.

The winner of the discus event was the first to step up to the mark. The throw was similar to today's—running forward with the javelin drawn back in the right hand, with the left arm extended, then releasing on the right foot. But one technical difference gave the ancients an advantage: A leather throwing thong, called the *agkyle,* was attached halfway down the javelin shaft, creating a loop into which athletes hooked two fingers. This gave extra leverage to the thrower's arm and the javelin a slight spin in the air, dramatically improving both power and accuracy (the throwing sticks of hunter-gatherers in Africa and Australia operate on a similar principle). Ancient authors claimed that throws of over 90 meters/270 feet were possible, about half the length of the Stadium and far beyond the modern record of 60 meters. In the late nineteenth century, tests of the ancient method using the *agkyle* were sponsored by the French government: With modest practice, untrained athletes were able to more than double their throwing distance, from twenty-five to sixty-five meters.

Again, accuracy was crucial for crowd safety. There are accounts of bystanders being accidentally impaled by javelins in the gymnasiums (in one case in Athens, a father sued an athlete for murder when his teenage son was speared and killed; the charge was dismissed because the boy had run across the firing range when he should not have). Miraculously, nobody ever seems to have suffered the same fate at Olympia.

ON ONE EDGE of the Stadium's field was a fifty-foot-long pit of softened earth called the *skamma*. For ancient spectators, the *halma*, or long jump, was the signature pentathlon event, the most sacred as well as the most difficult. It differed from its modern descendant in three ways: instead of a run-up, it commenced from a stationary starting position; contestants used weights; and it was accompanied by flute music.

The weights, called *halteres*, were not unlike dumbbells, with lumps at either end. They were held in both hands, and swung back and forth to provide momentum—"giving the athlete wings," as the coach Philostratus poetically put it. Made from lead, iron, or stone, they were curved for an easy grip, sometimes shaped like the handle of a telephone. While their use might sound superfluous, in 2002 researchers at England's Manchester Metropolitan University tested the effect of *halteres* on standing jumps, using modern athletes and computer simulations. They found that athletes using a pair of seven-pound weights in the Greek style could leap 6 percent farther than athletes jumping unassisted—adding seven inches to a nine-foot jump. And just as modern athletes experiment with technology to give themselves a subtle edge—swimmers using bodysuits, cyclists using

A long-jumper in mid-flight. To the left, an athlete exercises using the
halteres, *or hand weights; to the right, a judge uses a rod to measure the jump.*
(From an Athenian drinking cup, c. 500 B.C.)

ever-lighter and more efficient bikes—so the ancient Greeks
tested versions of the *halteres.* Excavated versions weighed anywhere from two and a quarter to ten pounds. Designs went in
and out of fashion: some *halteres* had more weight in the front, to
aid on the upswing, while cylindrical shapes were tried, indented
with finger grips.

For this delicate ancient sport, balance was key. The contestant took his position at "the threshold," or takeoff point—a base
at ground level, probably made of wood—crouching slightly.
The flutists began first, marking out a rhythm as he swung his
weighted arms back and forth. The athlete left the ground on the
upswing, then landed upright by swinging his arms backward.
It was imperative that the landing be clean—stumbling or traveling in the sand would result in a foul. Maintaining balance in
the long jump required constant practice. The flute music
helped concentration and style, and had been introduced, it was

said, to honor the god of music, Apollo, who had competed so successfully at Olympia (unfortunately this Pythian music has been lost, along with all but a few scraps of ancient music). Attendants measured the jumps with a stick called a *kanon;* as in the discus and javelin throw, every athlete was given five attempts.

How far did the ancients jump in this odd sport? A Greek epigram about the champion Phayllus declares that he leapt fifty-five feet around 480 B.C.—actually flying beyond the sandpit and breaking his leg (which led to the ancient expression "to jump beyond the *skamma,*" meaning a hyperbolic feat). A few years later, a Spartan named Chionis supposedly managed fifty-two feet. The distances were such that some modern historians have argued that the ancient "long jump" must in fact have been a triple or even quintuple jump; others insisted that it could only be a form of a hop, skip, and a jump. The truth, however, is that the superhuman jumps were probably poetic fabrications.

THE PENTATHLON WAS a grueling event. Some athletes dropped out in the course of the afternoon; others were eliminated. If nobody claimed three events, the finalists faced off in a wrestling match in the Sacred Grove. The ultimate victor had ribbons tied around his forehead and limbs, and was awarded an olive branch that he would carry with him until the close of the Games, when wreaths would be presented. He might dedicate his sports accessories to the gods and leave them in a temple, or he might commission specially crafted ceremonial discuses from local artists. The two finest examples found in Olympia are engraved with images of a long jumper on one side and javelin thrower on the other.

But all that lay in the future. As dusk settled over day two at Olympia, the serious business of partying could now begin.

X

To the Victors, the Feast

Just as the full moon dims the midnight stars with its brightness
So did the champion's body shine amongst the multitude of Greeks.
—BACCHYLIDES, VICTORY ODE FOR PENTATHLON
VICTOR AUTOMEDES, C. 450 B.C.

FLANKED BY TEMPLES and a tall hill, the Sacred Grove of
Zeus had the acoustics of an amphitheater. At dusk on day two,
the air began to ring with choruses of *tenella kallinike!* ("hail to
the champion!") as the victors, garlanded with flowers, were carried among the torchlit temples of the sanctuary. The winning
pentathlete and equestrian owners were much admired by the
crowd. But it was the celebrity owner of the winning four-in-
hand chariot who put on the most lavish, festive display. He was
usually rich, young, and flamboyant, and a triumph at Olympia
demanded that no expense be spared.

In 416 B.C., the glamorous Athenian Alcibiades—who, as we
recall, had entered seven chariots in the four-in-hand race—won
first, second, and fourth places, a feat unprecedented in Olympic
history, even by Greek kings. To mark his stunning success, Alcibiades decided to set a new standard in magnificence for his
victory banquet, feeding not only his supporters but the entire

Revellers celebrate a friend's success. (From an Athenian drinking cup, c. 450 B.C.)

teeming mass of spectators. As part of his sponsorship deal with the allies of Athens, the up-and-coming politician had cajoled financial support for his celebration: the city of Cyzicus provided sacrificial animals, the island of Lesbos the food and wine, Ephesus the banquet tent. Olympia had seen nothing like this lavish feast. Euripides, the greatest playwright of that time, wrote the victory ode for Alcibiades, and news of his triumph spread like wildfire throughout Greece.

The more typical victory banquet was an exclusive event—a private dinner for the victor, his family, and friends. (Xenophon describes one such gathering put on by the wealthy Callias for his young "boyfriend" who had just won a junior competition; it was a chummy affair attended happily by the boy's father, who typically accepted the social fiction that such pederastic relationships were chaste.) The most prestigious feasts would have as many as sixty or seventy guests, and cost up to ten thousand drachmas, as much as a skilled laborer's wages for thirty years.

Elegant marquees would glow with candlelight, and house re-clining couches that had been brought on wagon-back from distant cities. The same strict protocol for dining applied here as in the boudoirs of Athens or Miletus. The meal had to be completed before the drinking of wine could begin. Guests would lean back on their left elbow and eat with their fingers, using the right hand for most communal dishes and the left hand for bread. There were elaborate rules for the number of fingers used for each type of food and for its quantity, balancing an equal amount of bread with meat.

For the Greeks, banquets existed as a domain of male pleasure. Respectable women were rarely invited, but the beautiful hetaeras, or courtesans, were as carefully chosen as the food and wine for a successful party. Hosts would contact the upscale *pornoboskoi* ("prostitute shepherds," or pimps) for a handpicked selection of these charming women to provide witty conversation. Sex agents could also fill a banquet with voluptuous flute girls and handsome lyre players, who would often engage in erotic shows playing mythological lovers like Dionysus and Ariadne. The music is lost, but we know that tunes were usually variations on religious hymns such as "Zeus's Theme" or "Apollo's Chorus" (one Greek wit joked that the courtesans' favorite song should be called "The Grasping Hawk," referring to their ability to fleece their male admirers).

We have an idea of a hetaera's banquet demeanor from one of Lucian's dialogues, where a woman tutors her daughter on how to behave:

CROBYLE (THE MOTHER): First of all, a courtesan dresses like a lady, smartly and with good taste. She's gay with everybody— but doesn't giggle at just anything. She has a way of smiling sweetly and enticingly. Whenever she's invited to a dinner party as a paid escort, she never gets drunk—men can't stand you making a fool of yourself—and she never behaves like a pig and gorges herself. She handles her food with the tips of her fingers, doesn't smack her lips after a mouthful, and doesn't gobble away with both cheeks full. She drinks slowly, never gulping, but just sipping.

CORINNA (*incredulously*): Even when she's thirsty?

CROBYLE: *Especially* when she's thirsty. She never says more than she should, never makes fun of the other guests, and has eyes only for the man who's paying her. When she has to sleep with someone, she's isn't lewd, but never acts as if she doesn't care.

The availability of hetaeras at drunken victory banquets became the subject of many a lurid male fantasy. One apparently lovely courtesan named Neaera was at a riotous party for a charioteer in Delphi in 374 B.C., when her wealthy consort fell asleep in his chair. "Many had sex with Neaera while she was inebriated," notes the commentator, "even the servants of the host." Lucian describes a "rich Lesbian" hetaera at another banquet, who shaved her head, dressed like a man, and paid dancing girls for carnal favors. When respectable women were invited to these evening celebrations, they did not always find the atmosphere congenial. The female philosopher Hipparchia outwitted her fellow dinner guests in debate, but found her cleverness unappreciated: one male guest found he "had no defense against her logic, so started to pull off her clothes."

Efdipnias! ("Bon Appetit!")

WHAT WAS ON the menu at these wild Olympic feasts? Western haute cuisine, it could be argued, arrived in Greece from Sicily and southern Italy during the sixth century B.C. The large, sun-drenched island of Sicily was a land of plenty, its fields overflowing with plump livestock, juicy olives, and succulent cheeses; the pleasure-loving inhabitants of one southern Italian city, the Sybarites, became synonymous with hedonism itself. Sicilians wrote history's first cookbooks, and brought their skills back to the mainland, especially during the Olympic Games.

(Centuries later, the Greeks of southern Italy would teach Romans how to cook, but the pupils would soon outstrip their tutors in extravagance. The Romans' taste for highly seasoned and adventurous meals, thick with sauces, would ultimately render traditional Greek cooking as provincial and plain.) By the time of Socrates, in the fifth century B.C., infusions from Asia Minor and Africa had added to the culinary mix in Greece. Chefs at Olympia had to transport their own ingredients from afar, but this did not seem to moderate the level of indulgence. While Greeks normally agreed with the philosopher's dictum that one should eat to live, not live to eat, the Games were—for the superrich, at least—a time for giddy gourmandizing.

The typical fare at Olympia's banquets would have included such delicacies as roasted sow's womb, pork stewed with apples and pears, fried liver wrapped in lamb intestines, olives with mashed chickpeas, veal kebabs, whole piglets stuffed with the flesh of small birds, egg yolks, chestnuts, raisins, and spiced meat. Local hunters brought in freshly killed boars, stags, and gazelles from the surrounding mountains. Fish, the most beloved of Greek luxury foods, was sadly rare at Olympia because of its inland location and the summer heat. But gourmands, when they could get a catch barged up from the coast, went into paroxysms over the sea bass and red mullet, crustaceans and tuna, while the eel, it was said, "commands the field of pleasure." In an inspired example of early food writing, a chef catering a sports banquet is the happy recipient of a top-quality fillet: "Oh, what a fish was lying tender before me! What a dish I made of it! It wasn't drugged senseless with cheese sauces or window-boxed with dandifying herbs, but emerged from the oven naked as the day it was born. . . . The first of the guests to taste its delights leapt up and fled, taking the platter with him for a lap of the stadium, the others hot on his heels. I allowed myself a shriek of joy. . . . I have discovered the secret of eternal life; men already dead I can make walk again, once they smell this dish in their nostrils."

Sweets and nuts were mixed liberally throughout the meals, including ambrosial fruits, dates, fat figs, almonds, hazelnuts, Athenian honey cakes, and the favorite of all Greek sweets, cheesecake—the subject of many a learned treatise by ancient cooks.

AFTER THE MEAL, the interior would be swept, and the drinking could begin.

Wine was consumed as a communal act, not for intoxication but to fuel conversation, which Greeks regarded as the highest of all civilized pleasures. The banquet host acted as sommelier, mixing the wine with water in a large shared bowl—with slightly more water than wine—often adding infusions of salt water or perfume such as myrrh. We know that there were hundreds of varietals to choose from: almost every Greek colony had vineyards and exported its produce in distinctively shaped amphorae. Connoisseurs would weigh the merits of wines that were sweet, dry, or *autokratos,* in between; fragrant or odorless; "slender" or "fat." In one Athenian comedy, the god of the vine, Dionysus, ranks top wine producers. He favors the nectar from Thasos, with its "apple scent"; Mendean wine, so sweet that "the gods themselves wet their soft beds when they imbibe"; and a velvety Chian table wine that is mercifully "inoffensive—and painless."

The most intimate and cerebral drinking parties, with ten to fifteen guests, were the famous Greek symposia favored by rich students and university dons (who were definitely not bookworms, as the title of a dense volume by Athenaeus, *Deipnosophists,* "The Partying Professors," suggests). Here the wine and erotic dances helped stimulate lofty academic debate. Philosophy, science, poetry, geometry—nothing would escape the omnivorous intellectuals. Hosts could even buy "conversation guides" with handy lists of topics to draw on when chitchat flagged. Suitable discussion points included:

- Why did Homer call salt divine, but not oil?
- Why are the aged long-sighted?
- Why is *alpha* the first letter of the alphabet?
- Why does a piglet squeal on the way to sacrifice, while a sheep goes silently?
- How do you ward off the evil eye?
- In which hand was Aphrodite wounded by Diomedes in *The Iliad*?

Even though this elegant boozing was far removed from the casual quaffing enjoyed by the masses in their wagons, aristocratic decorum certainly frayed as the night progressed. Banquets would get out of control, as the large bowls, called kraters, went around, supplemented by drinking horns. Drunken party-goers succumbed to *paroinia,* the frenzy of intoxication. The playwright Eubulus advised wise guests to stop at the third cup, because "the fourth belongs to hubris, the fifth to shouting, the sixth to revel, the seventh to black eyes, the eighth to legal actions, the ninth to bile and the tenth to madness."

With a taste for debauchery as well as debate, professors led golden-haired youths in cavorting, playing practical jokes, and squandering their incomes on auctions of pretty young flute girls. At the height of the ecstasy, they often formed a version of the conga line called the *komos,* swaying around the Temple of Zeus with musicians by their side.

The Refuseniks

SOME OF THE greatest intellectuals of ancient life were avid sports fans, comprising a virtual *Who's Who* of Western civilization. According to many scholars, Plato got his nickname during his days as a virile young wrestler at the Isthmian games (from *platus,* probably meaning "broad-shouldered"; his real name was Aristocles). The playwright Sophocles, as well as being noted in the ring, was a famous handball player; the general Themistocles, who defeated the Persians, came to the Games of 476 B.C.; the mathematician Pythagoras may also have been a revered sports coach. But the Olympics did have their occasional critics. There had always been a modest but vocal undercurrent of anti-sports feeling among Greek thinkers. Understandably, in an age when Reason was paramount, some would argue the superiority of the mind over the body, and suggest that the national obsession with athletics was frivolous, even philistine.

The Cynic Diogenes, who traded repartee with Alexander the Great himself, was one of the most outrageous naysayers, and, in the fourth century B.C., he brought his attacks to the sports field itself. His best-documented demonstrations occurred at the Corinth games, when he grabbed a victory wreath from the prize table and put it on his own head, claiming that he was victor in the contest of life, and that spiritual rather than physical effort was more worthy of rewards. "Are those pot-bellied bullies good for anything?" he asked a gathering crowd. "I think athletes should be used as sacrificial victims. They have less soul than swine. Who is the truly noble man? Surely it is the one who confronts life's hardships, and wrestles with them day and night—not, like some goat, for a bit of celery or olive or pine, but for the sake of happiness and honor throughout his whole life."

Later, when he saw a sprinting champion being carried from the Stadium, Diogenes acidly noted that the rabbit and the antelope were the fastest of animals, but also the most cowardly. He later ran off with another victory wreath and put it on the head of a horse that had been kicking another horse, proclaiming it the victor in the *pankration* contest. Finally, Diogenes made reference to Hercules, the patron of athletes, who had cleaned the filthy Augean stables as one of the Twelve Labors—then Diogenes squatted on the ground and emptied his bowels, suggesting that competitors clean it up.

"At this the crowd scattered," we read, "muttering that Diogenes was crazy."

———

DIOGENES WAS ECHOING centuries of criticism. In the fifth century B.C., Euripides referred to athletes as the bane of Greece for their self-importance. Many Spartans thought the Olympic sports inefficient because they did not promote useful military skills. Centuries later, Roman moralists mocked the connection between the gymnasium and pederasty: Greek athletes, suggested the historian Tacitus, attracted only shirkers and perverts. But perhaps the most scathing antisports rant came from the second-century-A.D. doctor Galen who, in his career guidance pamphlet *On Choosing a Profession,* described athletes as the most useless of all citizens: "Everyone knows that athletes do not share in the blessings of the mind. Beneath their mass of flesh and blood, their souls are stifled as in a sea of mud. But the truth is that they don't enjoy the blessings of the body, either. Neglecting the old rules of health, which prescribe moderation in all things, they spend their lives like pigs—over-exercising, over-eating and over-sleeping. Their coaches fatten them and distort their limbs. Athletes rarely live to old age, and if they do, they are crippled by disease. Then they have neither health nor beauty. They become fat and bloated. Their faces are often flaccid and ugly, thanks to their boxing scars."

Eyes that have been gouged over the years go rheumy, Galen adds; battered teeth fall out; joints that have been incessantly twisted become arthritic.

"Even at their physical peak, their vaunted strength is useless to society. Can you fight wars with discuses in your hands? In fact, athletes are weaker than new-born babies."

Galen's solution? When choosing a profession, try becoming a doctor.

HARSH WORDS. BUT at Olympia, the antisports voices were faint—drowned out by the chorus of fans, who defended athletics on the grounds that they promoted endurance, physical beauty, and moral fiber. Apart from which, many Greek thinkers would have added as they cavorted drunkenly at victory banquets, the evenings were rather fun.

On a Sober Note

AS THE CONGA lines swayed around the Sacred Grove, there was one location where it was hard to keep a merry face. At the burial mound of Pelops—sealed off by a pentagonal wall—a gloomy funerary rite had been held after dark on day two (which for ancient Greeks was actually day three: the new day technically began at nightfall). A black ram had had its throat slit and its steaming blood poured into the earth, to nourish the hero in the Underworld. It was a reminder of man's sorry fate. In the classical era, pagans could draw little hope of life after death. Even heroes like Pelops were doomed to spend eternity in Hades, their spirits flitting batlike in the cold darkness. This melancholy prospect, it is recorded, often raised its ugly head at the happiest banquets, "a pang among the flowers" (as the Roman poet Lucretius said), to cast a pall over the exuberance.

Such dark thoughts had to be pushed aside. There was always another cup of wine to be had—and the parties would continue until dawn. The next morning, hungover revelers would cluster at the altars and sacrifice, rather forlornly, to the gods.

XI

The Sacred Slaughter

Greece is full of wonderful sights and stories, but nowhere is the aura of divinity so powerful as during . . . the Olympic Games.
—PAUSANIAS, *Description of Greece*, C. A.D. 160

IT TAKES A serious leap of our modern imaginations to remember that the pagan Olympic Games were devoted first to religion and only second to athletics: every sporting contest was dedicated to Zeus, and sacred rituals took up as much time as sports. In fact, asked to name the highlight of the Games schedule, a classical sports fan would not have chosen the chariot races, long jump, or even wrestling, but would instead have picked day three, when one hundred white oxen were sacrificed on a grand altar. This rite, coinciding with the rise of the full moon, was the Greeks' most important national ceremony, as spiritually profound as witnessing the secret mysteries of Eleusis or consulting Apollo's oracle at Delphi. Animal sacrifice was the central pagan practice, and at Olympia every moment was choreographed to show the unity of gods, men, and animals, while strict codes of conduct confirmed the hierarchy of all the mortals gathered. And yet, to modern eyes, the entire day seems a baffling mix of pomp and

The sacrifice rite. Two athletes are ready to roast chunks of meat on spits over the altar fire (where the head and horn of an ox are already cooking). The figure at left *oversees the ritual; at* right, *a flute player provides music, while the goddess Nike (Victory) hovers above the proceedings. (From a Greek amphora, c. 475 B.C.)*

butchery—as if Anglican High Mass were being performed in an abattoir.

Early on day three, spectators squeezed wherever they could around the Sacred Grove of Zeus. They tried to make themselves look respectable after two days of nonstop revelry; without baths, the dust was beginning to mat their hair, and bloodshot eyes squinted at the fierce rising sun. Many would have perched on stone fences and climbed olive trees for a view of the Council House, where the festival's largest and most colorful procession was gathering.

At first the scene resembled a village cattle market, with the one hundred lowing beasts, which were always donated by the host city of Elis, having to be whipped by shepherds into line. Sacred as it was, the practice of such a large-scale sacrifice could not help but be firmly embedded in earthly realities: Olympic officials in their robes of office tried in vain to keep their sandals clean, while the frankincense from the priests' swaying braziers fought a losing battle with the odors of terrified animals.

By the time the procession passed through a gate into the Sacred Grove, protocol had been enforced: Judges led, followed by priests and ambassadors bearing expensive gifts for Zeus, then the athletes, their family members and trainers, and finally the cows and bulls garlanded with flowers. The whole convocation did a turn around the perimeter for the crowds, before halting at the Great Altar of Zeus. On an elliptical base, a pyre of smoldering ashes over twenty feet high sent up a plume of smoke like a Hawaiian volcano; it stood before the Temple of Zeus, where an imposing bronze statue of the king of the gods, itself twenty-seven feet high, could watch the proceedings (unlike Christian ceremonies, performed in cathedrals, pagan rites were always conducted outside the temples). The chief priest took control and, with little introduction, an attendant came forward with sharpened blades.

The sacrifice procedure, as reconstructed by historians from ancient accounts, displayed a surprising reverence toward the animals about to be slaughtered—almost as if the Greeks wished to allay their residual carnivores' guilt. The first beast was brought to the altar, a carved slab of dark marble below the pyre. Flutists played calming melodies while the Olympic attendants stood in a circle around an animal, washed their hands in blessed water, then sprinkled drops of moisture on the animal's head—an act that symbolically made it nod in agreement to its honorable fate. A curl of hair was cut from its mane and tossed onto the altar fire. As the scent of singed hair wafted through the air, the priest below muttered an invocation to Zeus, while the attendants each took handfuls of barley grain—a symbol of fertility—and scattered them across the altar. Finally, the animal's head was held by assistants and its arterial vein cut so as to direct blood into a silver bowl. Accounts describe how the flutists broke into a high-pitched ululation, eerie and intense, then tapered off as the struggle ebbed and ceased.

The sheer volume of animal sacrifices performed around Greece in antiquity—it was the basic act of worship, repeated every time the favor of the gods was requested, whether before a battle, a voyage across the seas, a marriage, a political vote, or a business deal—meant that Greek temple attendants were experienced butchers. The oxen's thighs, as Zeus's portion of each beast, were sprinkled with wine and laid onto the fire, which was fed only with twigs of white poplar and olive branches. The crowd below watched with satisfaction as dark smoke billowed up to the skies, where it would give sustenance to the famished god. Later, the ashes would be mixed with water from the river Alpheus, then plastered onto the tall conical pyre, which thus increased in height at every Games.

The sacrificial production line had begun.

THROUGHOUT THAT THIRD morning, laborers would drag the remaining carcasses back to the Council House, where they were laid on slabs for an official named the "butcher-cook" to slice. They would be disemboweled, and the inedible intestines thrown into the river Alpheus. (It was said that a spring in Sicily magically erupted at this precise moment every four years, due to a subterranean connecting tunnel; another rumor was that a cup tossed into the Alpheus would magically float up there.) The carcass was then dissected into meal-sized portions. Ancient butchers had none of our modern regard for cuts based on tenderness, quality, or grain; they simply chopped a carcass geometrically. Even in cosmopolitan Greek cities, the only choice for customers at a market was between meat and offal. At Olympia, the chunks were placed in giant roasting pits, with the sweetmeats on metal skewers, an incipient form of shish kebab (and nicknamed by the Greeks of Egypt "obelisks," after the needle-like monuments).

It must have made an infernal scene. The sights and smells—blood soaking into the dry earth, the discarded skin and bone, the heat, the flies clustering in droves, the gore-covered attendants—would probably turn the stomach of a modern observer. But even in ancient Greece, there were vegetarians who rebelled at the slaughter. The Western world's first known animal-rights protest was made on day three of the Olympic Games in 460 B.C., by the philosopher Empedocles, who made his own life-sized bull out of dough, garnished it with expensive herbs, and distributed it among the onlookers. (Empedocles preached the doctrine of reincarnation, announcing that he himself had once been a fish and a bird, so eating flesh was tantamount to cannibalism.)

Few Greeks were won over. Meat was expensive, and sacrifices were the only time most citizens had a chance to savor it. On the evening of day three, spectators lined up for a public feast—for convenience, an impressive structure called the Southern Stoa would probably have been turned into a huge buffet with meat served on long trestle tables. The throngs would have arrived with their own plates. They could only hope for a small chunk of the sacrificial meat, and took whatever they were given, whether it was a mix of bone and gristle, a kidney, or a chunk of juicy filet mignon. The deliberate randomness symbolically reflected the equality of Greek worshipers. Officials called *oinoptai* were on hand to make sure that each citizen received an equal amount of wine. The aristocrats of Elis, who funded the feast, would no doubt have supplemented the meal with bread, and possibly vegetables, cheese, and the ubiquitous Greek barley porridge.

Plates and cups filled, the happy spectators filed back around the Temple of Zeus and the god's still-smoking altar, to dine al fresco beneath the summer stars.

The poet Pindar captures the exuberant scene: "The whole company raised a great cheer, while the lovely sight of the fair-faced moon lit up the evening, and then in joyful celebration the whole Sacred Grove of Zeus rang with the banquet song."

The Hairless Ones

INCIDENTALLY, THE AFTERNOON of day three, when spectators were waiting for the feast to be prepared, was the time allotted for the three boys' events—considered a low-key but pleasurable diversion. The contests, comprising running, wrestling, boxing, and the *pankration,* did not have the same prestige as men's competitions, but they were still extremely popular to watch. Cities feted the youngsters for their achievements; proud fathers would erect statues of their victorious sons and commission victory odes.

The exact cutoff age is uncertain, but "boys" appears to have included all adolescents from twelve to eighteen. Few twelve-year-olds may have made the final rounds in the boys' boxing, but on the running track, as with gymnastics today, child prodigies could defeat older teenagers: The twelve-year-old Damiscus of Messene won the boys' sprint in 368 B.C. Without birth certificates, well-developed teenagers might find themselves classified by the judges as men, as happened to a young boxer from Samos, who in 588 B.C. found himself sparring with full-grown adults and defeating them soundly.

Not everyone was enthusiastic. Aristotle argued that overzealous parents pushed their children too far in training. As proof, he noted that few adolescent Olympic champions were ever successful in the adults' categories once they came of age.

XII.

No Philistines in
the Stadium

Zeus, protect me from your guides at Olympia!
—VARRO, ROMAN ANTIQUARIAN AND INVETERATE SIGHTSEER,
C. 30 B.C.

IN TERMS OF artistic wealth, Olympia, with its gilded temples full of artwork and its illustrious sculpture gardens, contained more masterpieces per square foot than anywhere outside the Acropolis of Athens. The author Pausanias devotes fully two of the ten books of his second-century-A.D. travel guidebook, *The Description of Greece,* to the splendors of this national gallery, which lured erudite sightseers all year round. During the Games, however, with teeming multitudes of the pagan faithful on hand, the reverent buzz of art appreciation itself reached a passionate intensity. Even modestly educated Greek sports fans considered themselves connoisseurs of art, and judging from the ancient accounts, the act of tourism was pursued as vigorously as any blood sport during downtime between Olympic events. The city of Elis appointed volunteer guides—called *exegetai* or *mystagogi,* "those who explain the sacred places to strangers"—to assist the throngs. Pausanias says he got some of his juiciest stories from a helpful guide named Aristarchos, but other writers like Varro and Plutarch found the guides to be pushy and verbose, repeating their spiels by rote, ignoring questions, and inventing ludicrous tales. "Abolish lies from Greece," wrote Lucian, "and all the tour guides would die of starvation, since no visitor wants to hear the truth, even for free."

Today, we modern tourists are lucky to be able to view some of the most celebrated statues of ancient Olympia on location at its museum. (German excavators in the 1870s made a groundbreaking agreement with the Greek government to leave their finds inside the country, rather than purloining them as the British Lord Elgin had done with the Parthenon's marbles fifty years earlier, or as the French would later do in Delphi.) Of course, the displays represent the merest fraction of the artwork that sports fans once enjoyed; most of Olympia's masterpieces were looted or destroyed by Christians toward the end of the Roman Empire. Fortunately, we can use Pausanias' guidebook to visit the site as it looked then. Pausanias was the consummate ancient tourist, wealthy, learned, and somewhat pedantic, who worked his way across Olympia listing every frieze, sculpture, and relic. The afternoon of day three, while the boys' events were being held, must have been the ideal time for a little cultural tourism. After a light lunch of perhaps bread, fruit, and wine, a sightseer would give a few coins to one of the local guides—hoping not to be too exasperated by his prattle—and enter the fray.

The Glowering Icon

FIRST STOP, NATURALLY, was the Temple of Zeus, home to the most famous statue in the entire Mediterranean, one of the seven wonders of the ancient world. Today at Olympia, all that remains of the temple is a bare limestone platform. Archaeologists have recently raised a single fluted Doric column to its original height of sixty feet; the remains of thirty-three others, hewn from rough conglomerate, lie broken on the lawn like Lego blocks. In antiquity, the columns must have been magnificent

An artist's re-creation of Phidias' statue of Zeus, one of the Seven Wonders of the Ancient World.

and imposing—plastered and painted, supporting an entablature decorated with gilt bronze, red, and blue; inside, the floors were flagstones of black and white marble, with mosaics of Sirens.

An ancient visitor would have listened to his guide recite the temple measurements (250 feet in length, 95 breadth, 68 height,

Pausanias noted) before passing through a pair of giant bronze doors, only then to pause blinking in the darkness. Pagan temples were built facing east toward the sunrise, but there were no windows, so it took a few seconds to become accustomed to the gloom. As they pushed forward to the back chamber, however, they suddenly caught their breath: the bearded figure of Olympian Zeus loomed before them, forty feet high, presiding on his throne of cedar, glowering back at them in the flickering torchlight. Although the statue of Zeus has not survived, we know its details from innumerable ancient descriptions. The god's muscular flesh was carved from ivory, his robes plated in gold. In his right hand he held a scepter gleaming with gems, in his other, outstretched palm the winged statue of Victory. The vast statue was nearly too big for the temple. Zeus's head almost scraped the ceiling, noted the Greek geographer Strabo—if he wanted to stand, he would tear the roof off. But it was the god's grave expression, framed by his leonine tresses and flowing beard, that truly humbled the viewer. To the ancients, Zeus represented awesome, invincible power as well as sympathetic humanity. The sculptor Phidias, who created the statue, said that he had been inspired by a description of the god by Homer in *The Iliad.* Alexander Pope's translation of the verse conveys the grandeur:

> *(Zeus) spoke, and awful bends his sable brows,*
>   *Shakes his ambrosial curls, and gives the nod:*
> *The stamp of fate and sanction of the God.*
>   *High heaven with tremblings the dread signal took,*
> *And all Olympus to the centre shook.*

Pausanias himself found it hard to believe his guide's word that the statue was only forty feet tall: the sheer force of Zeus's presence made it seem immeasurably larger. Other audience reactions were just as hyperbolic. Beholding the image was a life experience, raved the philosopher Epictetus: No man could die happy who had not seen it. The Roman general Aemilius Paulus was "affected profoundly"—he felt that he had "beheld Zeus in person." Dio the Golden-Tongued said that the statue made humans forget their daily sorrows; even stray dogs who wandered into the temple were stunned into silence.

"Father and King," mumbled awestruck worshipers, "Protector of Cities, God of Friendship and Hospitality, Giver of Increase . . ."

Stunning though the image was, the temple was hardly a scene of monastic silence. Greeks treated statues of their gods as if they were alive. During the Olympics, priests dressed Zeus in judges' robes and were constantly rushing in from the Stadium to announce the results of each event. The workers called the Burnishers were forever massaging the statue with oil drawn from a black marble pool; it trickled through the statue's interior along minuscule channels created by Phidias to transmit the preservative fluid like arteries in a human body. And the temple floor was crowded with supplicants who stood before Zeus with outstretched arms, their heads barely reaching the god's knees, arguing their cases out loud—athletes asking to be blessed with victory, villagers praying for assistance with the winter rain, politicians asking for success in diplomacy, soldiers seeking benedictions. Scattered everywhere were gifts and offerings—miniature statues, golden horns of plenty, shields and trophies, even mounds of human hair: Greek teenagers emerging from puberty traditionally left one of their locks to Zeus.

The building had a mezzanine level, so visitors could admire Phidias' artwork at head height. This also allowed them to whisper their more personal requests into Zeus's shell-like ear—trying to avoid vertigo as they did so, since they were teetering up as high as a three-story house. The supreme deity took a briskly bureaucratic attitude toward the prayers of mortals, requiring worshipers to fill out small papyrus pledges that stated what gift the god would be given—usually sacrifices or donations of money—if the wish was granted. The pledge would then be affixed with wax to the walls of the temple; the dark interior was covered with these scraps, like a subterranean cave lined with fluttering moths.

Phidias was so famous and beloved—he had also created a giant image of Athena for the Parthenon of Athens—that there was a modest "artist trail" at Olympia for his admirers to follow. The workshop where the maestro had built his statue of Zeus had been preserved for posterity, and Pausanias inspected it at leisure. (Today, the workshop is still in good condition at Olympia. In 1958, German archaeologists found bronze tools, fragments of ivory and glass—evidently chips from a sculpture—and even a black-glazed drinking vessel with the inscription *Pheidio eimi,* "I belong to Phidias.") Ancient tourists were then shown a commemorative jar marking the spot struck by a lightning bolt when Phidias had asked Zeus for a sign of his approval, around 420 B.C., of the newly completed statue. True Phidias fans might have rushed back for a closer look at the image. Hidden on one hand was a snatch of graffiti supposedly inscribed by Phidias himself, dedicated to his teenage boyfriend: "Pantarkes is beautiful."

Celebrity in the ancient world had its dangers, even for artwork. In A.D. 40, the deranged Roman emperor Caligula ordered the statue of Zeus decapitated, and his own head placed on Zeus's shoulders. Heaven made short work of the blasphemy. When workmen approached the temple, a deafening peal of laughter rang out, nearly shattering their eardrums. The boat sent from Italy to fetch the statue was then struck by lightning. Caligula took the divine hint and left the statue of Zeus alone, but of course nobody in Greece was surprised when, the following year, the emperor was murdered.

Unfortunately, we cannot share the ancients' awe today. The illustrious statue was finally moved by a Christian emperor to Constantinople in the fourth century A.D., where it perished in a palace fire about a century later.

VISITING ZEUS WAS merely the beginning of a busy afternoon for ancient tourists. Every spare inch of the temple was covered with paintings and friezes illustrating episodes from Greek myth. The statue's cedar chair was engraved with images of the Amazons, the warrior women of the East. Interior walls were covered with *metopes*—stone reliefs recounting the Twelve Labors of Hercules. Outside, the temple's eastern pediment was decorated with a magnificent set of statues depicting a scene from Pelops' bloody chariot race. The western pediments showed the figures of drunken centaurs trying to carry off women at the wedding festival of the Lapiths. (The two groups of statues, miraculously, survive and are on display at the Olympia museum today, although without the garish colored backdrops that made them stand out in antiquity; the gables behind the statues, archaeologists believe, were bright blue.)

Highlights in the Sacred Grove vicinity included the statue of Nike (Victory) taking flight atop a twenty-five-foot pillar carved by Paionios in 421 B.C.; mythological bric-a-brac in the Temple of Hera, including a Sphinx with a smiling female face; and shields captured from the Persians during the battle of Marathon. Like all ancient tourists, Pausanias was even more excited by actual relics of mythology. In the temple of Hera, he gazed upon the ivory horn of the goat Amalthea, who had suckled the infant god Zeus. Standing in a nearby field was a single charred wooden pillar, a remnant from the palace of the sadistic King Oinomaos, who had been killed in the chariot race with Pelops; after the king's demise, it had been blasted to smithereens by a lightning bolt from the gods. Pausanias was disappointed on his visit that the enormous shoulder blade of the hero Pelops himself, which had been fished from the waters near Troy by fishermen, had not survived for his admiration. Whalebones and dinosaur fossils were often put on display by the Greeks as physical evidence of heroes, giants, and Titans. ("I suppose the bone moldered away with age," Pausanias writes resignedly in his guidebook, "from the corrosive action of the salt water in which it had been sunk so long.")

The Lure of the Water

IN THE CRUSHING heat of the afternoon, visitors must have cast longing eyes toward the western edge of the sanctuary, where they knew a large swimming pool existed. Olympia was unique in Greece for having such an asset—about twenty-four meters long by sixteen meters wide, and around 1.6 meters (five feet) deep, roughly half the size of an "Olympic pool" today. But it was used for recreation rather than competitions, and probably open only to VIPs and athletes. It is strange that, among a people who even held eating races at dinner, swimming was one of the only pursuits that was *not* elevated to a competition, except in one small, provincial city called Hermione.

To the Greeks, who grew up surrounded by rivers, lakes, and the pellucid waters of the Aegean, swimming was as natural as walking, and unworthy of contests. To be unable to swim—at least among the free male population—was as much a sign of an uneducated person, or barbarian, as being illiterate. From vase paintings, it appears that their favorite stroke was freestyle, although they were familiar with the sidestroke, backstroke, and breaststroke, and would dive from sheer cliffs. City elders certainly recognized the practical value of swimming for maritime powers. At the great naval battle of Salamis, the Greeks suffered remarkably few casualties because their sailors could all escape porpoiselike to shore, while the unfortunate Persians sank like stones. Tales abound of Greek sailors dodging arrows by swimming underwater or using divers to destroy underwater traps. Rowing, however, and various boat races became very popular at municipal games. In Athens, regattas were held in boats with crews of up to eight men—and even races of full-blown military ships. Triremes with triple banks of oars would compete off Cape Sounion, where a magnificent Temple of Poseidon stood sentinel, and priests would sacrifice giant tuna, pouring their black blood on the altar.

XIII

To Race with Immortals

The track below his feet scarcely feels him as he sprints:
His feet tread tenuous air, the rare steps hover
And leave no prints in the smooth sand . . .
—STATIUS, *Thebais*, FIRST CENTURY A.D.

THE CLIMAX OF the Games, from the athletic standpoint, was day four. The events started with the footraces. Running was the oldest of Olympic sports, with all the cachet of Greek tradition behind it; indeed, for the first thirteen Olympiads, it had been the *only* Olympic sport—the *stadion*, a sprint along the straight 210-yard Stadium track, which had first been won in 776 B.C. by Coroibos, a cook from Elis. In 724 B.C., a double-lap race (the *diaulos*) was introduced, followed in 720 B.C. by a twenty-four-lap long-distance race (the *dolichos*), about three miles.

Loneliness of the *Dolichos* Runner

IN THE PURPLE light before dawn, at least eighty athletes, twenty in each race and more for heats in the shorter races, would have entered their long waiting room next to the Stadium. As they stretched and oiled up in the cool morning air, they would hear the din of arriving spectators become an unmistakable roar, as the crowd filled the embankments to overflowing, many of the spectators still nibbling on their breakfast bread dipped in wine. Finally, the trumpet blasts summoned the first twenty contestants into the so-called Secret Tunnel, where they would one by one be brought before the judges. The poet Statius describes one runner, "tawny with rich oil, sleek and glossy," emerging into the Stadium: "His limbs shone forth, and all his graceful frame was revealed, his fine shoulders and chest as smooth and comely as his cheeks, so that his face was utterly overshadowed by his body's beauty." The ideal candidates for the first race, the *dolichos,* or long-distance event, should, according to Philostratus, "have powerful necks and shoulders like the candidate for the pentathlon, but they should have light, slender legs . . . They run almost as if they were walking."

The contestants who had already been introduced performed their final warm-up exercises: "Now they sink down with bent knees," says Statius, "now smite with loud claps their slippery chests, now ply their fiery feet in short spurts and sudden stops." They then approached the marble *balbis.* Every modern visitor to Olympia has marveled at these original starting lines, which lie at each end of the Stadium. Footraces were arranged so that the final lap would be run toward the west—a throwback to the earliest days of the Games, when Olympia had been an open field and athletes raced to the altar of Zeus. This meant that long-distance and double-lap runners started at the east end, which had the practical advantage of keeping the rising sun behind them during the final dash. The twenty runners drew lots from a silver urn to choose a lane. Each one was separated by a wooden post every four feet and was marked with a letter from the Greek alphabet; strung before the runners, at chest height, was a taut rope.

As with the chariot races, ancient footraces provoked Greek engineers to feats of technological innovation—in this case, by creating a fascinating, spring-loaded contraption called the *hys-*

Sprinters, looking frenzied in mid-flight. (From an Athenian prize amphora in the Panathenaic Games, c. 525 B.C.)

plex, which worked as a starting gate. Archaeologists have debated for decades the exact details of its workings, using the physical evidence at Olympia and literary descriptions. The favored model has the rope strung between two wooden arms, one at each end of the starting line. These arms were part of twin mechanisms that worked on the same principle as the catapult or mousetrap: When the arms were cocked, the rope maintained a taut barrier in front of the athletes, but a release trigger would slam the arms and the rope to the ground. A single official standing behind the starting line could release both at once by pulling on two cords. (An alternative design, recently proposed by researchers at the University of Pennsylvania, suggests that the rope did not slam downward but was spring-loaded to fly above the runners' heads.)

When the judges gave the nod, the twenty runners slipped their toes into the marble starting sills—the parallel grooves meant that one foot was only about seven inches ahead of the

Long-distance runners loping along the course. (From a Panathenaic amphora, dated 333 B.C., by the name of the Athenian magistrate engraved on its flanks.)

other—and took their stances. Instead of assuming the modern crouch, ancient contestants stood upright, leaning slightly forward, arms outstretched, like divers ready to jump. The herald blew a trumpet, and at the cry of *ápete!* the starting mechanism was released, and the rope barrier sprang open. Statius writes that "the runners nimbly dashed away, their naked forms gleaming upon the plain. One might deem them so many arrows shot by hosts of pouring Parthians." Those who made false starts, or were tangled in the cord, would be thrashed by the official policemen and the race would have to be restarted.

There were twenty-four laps, backward and forward along the straight running track. This, of course, was different from modern stadiums, where athletes run around a curved track. The ancient design required turning posts: for the *diaulos,* or double-lap race, the twenty runners would be given individual posts, which

An artist's re-creation of the hysplex, *or starting gate for running races, as hypothesized by some researchers. When the trigger is released by an official* (right), *a catapult mechanism slams the barrier to the ground.*

they tightly rounded to the left. But for the twenty-four-lap race, it appears that a single, solid column was used, and athletes thundered around it in a pack, like horses at the Hippodrome. This post evidently had a wide stone base to prevent runners from grabbing it and swinging themselves around, but the crowded turns were still an opportunity for chicanery: According to Lucian, some "worthless competitors" would trip other runners, block their paths, or cut inside the post. Poets include tales of runners even grabbing competitors by the hair to slow them down.

No wonder this awkward design was replaced by an oval for modern sports. And yet, there was one heroic attempt to adapt the classical running track for contemporary needs: The Roman-era stadium in Athens, once used for the city's ancient Panathenaic Games, was renovated for the 1896 Olympics and the straight track given curves at each end. But the turns were too cramped for modern athletes, reducing their performances. (Today, it is no longer used for track events, except as a rousing finishing point for the annual Marathon to Athens run.)

LONG-DISTANCE RUNNERS depicted on Greek vase paintings seem familiar to us today, loping along with their arms close to their sides in a relaxed jogging rhythm. But ancient contestants relied on more than physical conditioning. In the last lap, they would mentally call on the gods to help spur them on. Homer recounts a multilap race held during the siege of Troy, when Odysseus ran so close behind Ajax that "his feet landed in Ajax's tracks before the dust had settled, and his breath beat down on Ajax's head as he sped on." When they reached the final stretch, Odysseus

> *Said a silent prayer to gray-eyed Athena:*
> *"Hear me, goddess, and don't fail my feet now."*
> *Pallas Athena heard his prayer*
> *And made his hands and feet light.*

At Olympia, the twenty-four-lap *dolichos* took about fifteen minutes. At the early hour, it seems that drowsy spectators did not pay full attention to the race, using the time to gather their wits and settle into the Stadium. The relative lack of spectacle may be why long-distance running brought out the bad jokes in ancient Greece. Two survive:

A man named Charmos once came in seventh in a six-man race. One of his friends was running alongside the track, barking encouragement from the sidelines, but still beat him. "And if Charmos had had five friends," goes the joke, "he would have finished twelfth."

A runner named Marcus was so slow that the judges mistook him for one of the stone statues around the Stadium. As night fell, they locked up the gates—and when they came back the next morning, Marcus had still only finished the first lap.

Perhaps you had to be there.

AS WE KNOW, the ancient Greeks never had a "marathon" race of twenty-six miles (they considered the three-mile *dolichos* a sufficiently long-distance contest). The event is a modern invention, inspired by two stories about the Persian Wars.

In 490 B.C., when the Athenians learned that a Persian army had landed at Marathon to attack their city, they sent a runner—most manuscripts use the name Philippides—to request assistance from Sparta, 153 miles away. Philippides was one of the *hemerodromoi,* or foot couriers, who carried messages around the rugged mountain trails of Greece (and so, the historian Herodotus opines, "he was used to doing this sort of thing"). He covered the distance in less than thirty-six hours—a superhuman effort, although on a mountaintop en route he had a delirious vision of the god Pan, who sprang from a grotto and asked him why the Athenians did not make offerings to him with any regularity. The second story is more famous, but quite possibly apocryphal. After the battle of Marathon, a courier—who some say was named Philippides, and a few even suggest was the same man—dashed from the battlefield to take news of the Greek victory to Athens. He staggered before the city magistrates, gasped out the words "Rejoice! We won!" then collapsed and died. True or not, this 26.3-mile distance from Marathon to Athens has become engraved in stone as the length of modern marathon races around the world.

The ancients certainly did admire feats of endurance. Special honor went to Drymos of Argos, winner of the *dolichos* in the 320 B.C. Olympics, who immediately decided to run the eighty miles to his hometown of Epidaurus to announce his victory—and arrived there on the same day. He boasted of the feat on the base of his statue at Olympia, as "an example of my manliness." In Roman times, athletes would jog for an entire day around the Circus Maximus to prove their skill, sometimes covering 150 miles without a break (an eight-year-old boy is even said to have covered seventy miles one long afternoon).

Were these feats even physically possible? Many scholars were unsure. Then, in 1982, a British RAF officer and athlete decided to test Herodotus' claim that Philippides had run the 153 miles from Athens to Sparta by repeating the feat himself. He and a friend covered the distance in just under thirty-six hours—inspiring the start of the annual Spartathlon race in Greece along the same route. This "ultra-marathon" race is the longest on the planet, run overnight from Athens to Sparta every September through the mountains of Arcadia. As the winner touches the statue of King Leonidas in Sparta, he is crowned with an olive wreath by two local girls and then whisked to the hospital for a medical checkup. The record is currently held by a Greek, Yannis Kouros, at twenty hours, twenty-five minutes.

Flight of the Sprinter

AFTER WATCHING THE long *dolichos,* the crowd at ancient Olympia would no doubt have been pleased to see the pace pick up with the two-lap race, which was named after the *diaulos,* or double pipe. It was over in a matter of minutes. Then came the race everyone was waiting for. The *stadion,* or single-lap sprint, was, in a sense, the blue ribbon event of the entire Games. The Olympiad would be named after the victor, and since history itself was dated by the Games, it was he who thus gained the purest dose of immortality. (Historians would refer to, say, 457 B.C., by our dates, as "the third year of the eightieth Olympiad, when Ladas of Argos won the *stadion*"—rather a mouthful, but resonant.)

Just as it is today, the race was a crowd-pleaser—short, sharp, and dramatic. The Stadium was by now fully bathed in morning light as the athletes took their places at the western starting line, the Temple of Zeus looming ahead of them. Philostratus says that the best *stadion* runners should be tall, but not too tall: "Excessive height . . . lacks firmness, like a plant which has shot up too high. . . . They should be solidly built, the chest should be smaller than normal and should contain sound inner organs, the knees must be limber, the calves straight, the hands above average size." They should not be as bulked up as the wrestlers, he stresses, "for oversized muscles are fetters to speed."

Again, there would have been twenty competitors for the final. (If there were more contenders for this popular event, heats of four runners each were held first, organized by lot.) The spring-loaded starting gate was cocked—the judges took their places at the finishing line—and they were off, apparently running so fast that poets repeatedly refer to famous sprinters "leaving no tracks in the sand." When historians in the nineteenth century examined vase paintings of this event, they proclaimed the ancient sprinting style to be wild, anarchic, even grotesque. The runners' flailing limbs, one author complained, made them look as if they were inelegantly "advancing by leaps and bounds with arms and hands spread-eagled." But the Victorians did not allow for artistic license—the right arm raised with the right leg is a stylization to achieve graphic balance and symmetry. Today, apart from this sleight of hand, they seem quite accurate representations—strikingly suggestive of a sprinter captured in photographic motion.

For the three judges waiting at the finishing line, the *stadion* was almost as difficult as the horse races to adjudicate: In the age before photo finishes, arguments about errors and partisanship occurred. In one notorious case in 396 B.C., the three umpires of Elis were divided two to one over a result, favoring a local Elian over an outsider from Ambracia. Normally, the majority ruling would carry the day without question. But this time, protests were lodged with the Olympic Council, which overturned the decision and fined the two officials for dishonesty—a rare instance of Olympic judging being dishonored.

AS FOR THE running times, Greek references are typically cryptic. Ancient writers might say that one champion could catch hares on foot, while another outpaced a horse from Coronea to Thebes. Unfortunately, they never became more specific—and not just because sundials and water clocks were incapable of precision. The Greeks simply did not share our modern passion for comparing performances. Their archives did not register the longest javelin throws or discus toss, either. Instead, the Greeks accrued "records" by the sheer number of an individual's victories—opting for quantity rather than quality.

The greatest Olympic runner of all time by this yardstick was Leonidas of Rhodes, who won all three footraces in the Games of 164 B.C. and was given the honorary title *Triastes,* or "triple crowned." He went on to repeat the achievement in each of the next three Olympiads, clocking up a staggering total of a dozen wreaths. Leonidas was said to run "with the speed of a god"; on his home island, his compatriots took the accolade literally and worshiped him as an immortal. It was around this time that athletes began to number their victories in obsessive detail on memorials—totting up an entire lifetime's worth of triumphs in sacred, prize, and local games.

Any idea of gauging the speed of ancient runners becomes even more complicated when we learn that there were not even standardized lengths for the stadiums around Greece. Every running track was "six hundred feet," but this was literally six hundred times the foot size of whoever first walked it. At Olympia, according to myth, Hercules had simply put one foot in front of the other six hundred times, so that "six hundred Olympic feet" were 210 yards, or 192.28 meters. Delphi's mountaintop running track, while quoted as "six hundred feet," was a mere 177.5

meters long, while the track at Pergamum, whose founder must have had elephant feet, was a whopping 210 meters—nearly 10 percent longer than Olympia's.

One historian dryly notes that "time records would have been useless, even if the Greeks had had stop watches."

VICTORY RIBBONS AND pine branches were awarded to the three triumphant runners—they would carry them until the olive wreaths were presented in the closing ceremonies—and almost instantly the crowd turned its thoughts to the afternoon events. Running was revered for its traditional status, but the most thrilling of the nonequestrian events were the "heavy sports" of wrestling, boxing, and the *pankration*. These were also known as the "combat sports," evoking their connection to the military ethos of the Greek city-states and the endless warfare that hovered around the fringes of the Games.

XIV

Javelins into Spears

IF THE NADIR of the modern Olympics came at Munich in 1972—when eleven Israeli athletes were kidnapped by members of the PLO, two executed, and the rest killed in a botched rescue attempt—the ancient equivalent was in 364 B.C., as the sacred Games of Zeus were interrupted by a military assault in the middle of a wrestling match.

The bloodbath that ensued was the tragic result of a thousand-year-old grudge, rooted in obtuse mythology. The town of Pisa, located around four miles from Olympia, had long believed that the sanctuary had been usurped by the Elians in darkest antiquity, and had watched the growing prestige of the festival with ill-concealed resentment. Around 365 B.C., when the Elians foolishly abandoned their policy of neutrality and became embroiled in Greek squabbles, the Pisatans saw their chance. In alliance with the Arcadians, residents of the mountainous interior of the Peloponnesus who had no love for the city of Elis, they occupied Olympia with troops—and to celebrate the new regime, they decided to avenge generations of humiliation by hosting the Games themselves.

Disturbing as this situation was, contestants and spectators gathered from around Greece to attend the 364 B.C. Olympics as usual. But the Elians could not let this insult stand, and decided to attack Olympia itself, at the moment of maximum impact—late in the afternoon of day two, during the final round of the pentathlon, while the tiebreaking wrestling match was actually in progress. We can only imagine the chaos at Olympia as word spread of the Elian army approaching along the Sacred Way. The Pisatans, the Arcadians, and their allies took up defensive positions along the banks of the Cladeus River; archers were placed on the roofs of temples. Perhaps a total of some five thousand troops were deployed on the two sides around Olympia—opposing lines of hoplites, armored foot soldiers with long spears, backed by a massed contingent of cavalrymen.

According to the historian Xenophon, the defenders did not expect much of a fight: The Elians were regarded as hopelessly soft thanks to their centuries of peace, and truly abject soldiers. But the attack, when it came, was shockingly successful. The enraged Elians shattered the Arcadian defense, pushing forward into the Sacred Grove of Zeus itself, where bloody hand-to-hand combat ensued. The spectators apparently treated the battle like an exciting sports event. According to the author Diodorus, crowds "still wearing their festive robes, with wreaths and flowers in their hair" watched the fighting from the sidelines, "impartially applauding the doughty deeds performed on both sides."

The Elians were carrying the day until "they were pelted from the roofs of the arcades, the senate house, and the great Temple of Zeus itself," forcing them to retreat to their camps at sunset. The defenders panicked. Working nonstop through the night, they tore down the wooden booths and barracks from the spectators' tent-city to create a bristling stockade around Olympia. It is a testament to the size of the shantytown that the barricade was large enough to make the Elians abandon their attack when they saw it the next morning. Ancient sources do not catalog the casualties of this unique battle, but they do relate that soon afterward, the Arcadians began pillaging Olympia's treasuries to pay their mercenaries. It seems that many Greeks were shocked by the sacrilege, and fretted that the gods would exact retribution for their petty mortal bickering, sending plagues or ill luck. Pressure was brought to bear on the Pisatans by their allies to drop their claim.

In a genuine example of pagan religion restoring law and order, the next Games were sheepishly handed back to Elis and the victors of 364 B.C. struck from the record.

The Scourge of Politics

WITH THEIR ENDLESS rounds of alliance and war, the ancient Greeks were like a brilliant but pathologically dysfunctional family. They shared a common language, with minor regional dialects; they all worshiped Zeus, Apollo, and the other Olympian gods; they dismissed anyone in the outside world as rude *barbaroi,* barbarians. But almost nothing could stop the Greeks from bickering among themselves. They were passionate about their regional independence, their armies marching back and forth across the sun-blasted ravines in a dizzying cycle of petty feuds. Only one thing brought the Greeks together, and gave a peaceful outlet to their rivalries: athletics. It was the glue of the Aegean world. But the Games weren't so much a celebration of peace as a substitute for open violence—and it is hardly surprising that politics and machinations of all kinds affected the festival.

Along with sporting statues, trophies of conflict littered the Stadium and the sanctuary of Olympia—shields with signs crowing "Athens won this from the Argives" or "Boeotia robbed this from the Corinthians." Statues and plaques were erected to commemorate battles (the famous statue of Nike, far from being a memorial of peace, was erected on a twenty-five-foot-high pillar by the Messenians to commemorate their victory in a vicious war with the Spartans). At times of high tension, spectators at the Games behaved with little more fraternal affection than British soccer fans today, breaking into open brawls.

The battle of 364 B.C. was simply the most spectacular of many political imbroglios in the history of the Games. There were also embargoes: The Spartans were banned from attending in 424 B.C., during the Peloponnesian War (one Spartan citizen, who slipped into the Games pretending to be Boeotian, was publicly whipped). Four years later, the Spartans got into further trouble by mounting a military campaign with one thousand soldiers in the middle of the Sacred Truce (they were fined one *mina* per soldier involved, perhaps $5 million in today's buying power). In 380 B.C., the Athenians boycotted the Olympics when one of their athletes was caught in a corruption scandal.

Even during less violent times, politics boiled furiously. Diplomats took advantage of the Sacred Truce to negotiate peace treaties, the terms of which were engraved on tablets and hung

Poised for battle: Greek warriors await an attack in the film The 300 Spartans *(1962).*

on temple walls. Rabble-rousing speakers addressed the crowds on the key issues of the day. In 388 B.C., an orator named Lysias gave what subsequently became known as his "Olympic Oration" against the tyrant Dionysius of Syracuse, who had arrived with an entourage from Sicily to observe the Games; the mob (who as we know was already appalled at the bad quality of the king's poetry) went on a rampage and sacked the king's luxurious tent.

As befitted its social and cultural importance within Greece, Olympia became a political showcase for foreign conquerors. When King Philip of Macedon subjugated the Greeks in 338 B.C., he raised a circular monument in the sacred precinct of Zeus called the Philippeion; filled with ivory and gold statues of the Macedonian royal family, it was a permanent reminder of Greece's humiliation. Philip's son Alexander the Great, who regarded Olympia as the capital of the Greek world, had his military victories announced in the sanctuary—as well as the happy news, in 324 B.C., that he was divine. In 146 B.C., the conquering Romans placed trophies from sacked Greek cities in the Temple of Zeus itself; later, the first emperor Augustus turned Olympia's original Temple of Rhea into a shrine to Rome, complete with a statue of himself dressed up as Zeus.

And yet, we can't be entirely cynical about the amicable possibilities of the Games. There were times when the Olympics did inspire Greeks to moments of sanity.

The Dream of Peace

WHEN ANCIENT HISTORIANS choose to become dewy-eyed about the Olympic Games, they use as their apogee the festival of 476 B.C. First of all, it was an extraordinary moment in history: a few years earlier, the Greeks had united to miraculously defeat the invading Persian Empire, a David and Goliath act that would define the division between East and West to the present day. In Italy, meanwhile, the Greek colonies had combined to defeat an invasion by the Carthaginians. Every important figure in Greece, including the victorious generals of these campaigns such as Themistocles, converged on the Olympic Games to celebrate the dawning of a new era, and an idealistic vision of Hellenic cooperation germinated. The trophies that had previously commemorated wars between the city-states were removed from the Stadium, and it must have seemed possible to those present that the Greeks would never plunge themselves into fratricidal war again. The potential implicit in the sacred peace of the Games seemed poised to save Greece.

That episode of unity was painfully brief. Fifty years later, Greece would be mired in the Peloponnesian War, a pitiless conflict that descended to unheard-of levels of savagery. But in those five decades between the end of the Persian Wars and the start of that suicidal conflict, a Golden Age had flared across the land, led most famously by Athens under Pericles—a brilliant statesman who was able to guide the unruly democracy to momentary greatness. Pericles fostered a spasm of creativity whose brief but intense brilliance would not be seen again in Europe until Renaissance Florence. Olympia benefited enormously from a building program and new masterpieces, while astonishing intellectual advances—in drama, art, science, philosophy, history, political science, mathematics—were made by a collection of geniuses around Greece.

And yet, despite its brevity, the vision of Greek unity remains, an article of faith in modern Olympic iconography, and even invoked in the formation of the United Nations.

XV.

The Forgotten Amazons

*O Sparta! I give thanks for the excellence of your wrestling school,
but even more for the blessings of your Gymnasium for Virgins,
where the girls may be admired quite naked as they wrestle
amongst the men.*

—PROPERTIUS, ROMAN POET, FIRST CENTURY B.C.

THE ANCIENT OLYMPICS were the ultimate venue for Greek
male bonding. Although unmarried women were permitted to
attend (Pausanias is clear on the point), and female prostitutes
roamed the tent-city, testosterone levels must have been as high
as in a Turkish bathhouse. Only one married woman was allowed
to enter the sanctuary during the Games: a priestess of Demeter,
the Greek goddess of fertility, who sat on a stone throne on the
north bank of the Stadium. (The seat was found during excavations, and can still be seen at the site; the presence of the priestess may have been a tradition left over from the festival's origins
as an agrarian rite. Naturally, this was quite a coveted position
amongst high society Greek women. In the second century A.D.,
for example, it was held by Regilla, wife of the philanthropist
Herodes Atticus, who had pumped millions into renovations at
Olympia.) The punishment for any other married woman who

dared to "defile the Games by their presence" was to be flung to
her death from a nearby cliff—although this ruling was never
carried out, even in the notorious case already mentioned from
404 B.C., when a matron from Rhodes cropped her hair, put on a
trainer's tunic, and slipped into the stands to watch her son compete. Unfortunately, in her excitement at the boy's victory, she
leaped over the trainer's barrier, catching her tunic's fringe and
exposing her deception. The judges let her off with a warning
because she came from a famous sporting family—her husband
and father had both been Olympic champions. Still, married
women who came to the Games did not miss out entirely. There
was a view of the Stadium from the south side of the river

*A female runner in
Amazon-style tunic,
with one breast exposed.
(Artist's impression,
taken from a surviving
Roman copy of a fifth-
century-B.C. Greek
bronze statue.)*

Alpheus, and it is quite possible that the camping conditions were more pleasant than on the cramped, male-dominated fields.

While women were forbidden to compete at Zeus's Games, Greek girls (probably between twelve and eighteen) were given their own separate sporting event, which was held at Olympia and dedicated to Zeus's consort Hera, and included footraces in which girls raced in short tunics with their right breast exposed. The sole surviving description of this extraordinary gathering, which echoed prenuptial initiation rites in other parts of Greece, is provided by Pausanias in his guidebook *The Description of Greece,* and the details are tantalizingly few. We know that the events were limited to three sprints between virgin girls of different ages. They ran along the same track in the Olympic Stadium as the men, but it was shortened by a sixth, to 160 meters. Historians speculate that their unusual dress, exposing one breast, evoked the Amazon women of myth: This race of female superwarriors, said to live in Asia Minor near the Black Sea, were believed to have cauterized their right breasts so as not to impede their javelin throwing.

The origins of Hera's Games are also shrouded in folk memory. Pausanias reports that the festival was instituted in darkest antiquity, by the lovely Hippodameia in thanksgiving for her wedding to the hero Pelops (who had, as we know, killed her father in the famous chariot race for her hand). Hippodameia celebrated the sports event with the assistance of sixteen matrons—and ever since, the Games of Hera had been hosted by the married women of Elis, the most honored sixteen of whom were chosen to knit a ceremonial robe to be worn by the goddess Hera's statue in her temple at Olympia. This cadre of grandes dames also organized festivals in Elis for Dionysus, the god of adult women, and choruses for various local heroines (one of whom, Physcoa, had born the god a son).

Some elements of the festival of Hera—which appears to have been formalized around 580 B.C. in a treaty inscribed by the Elians—echoed the men's festival. It was held at Olympia every fourth year. Victors were crowned with sacred olive wreaths and given a portion of a sacrificed cow at a final banquet. They were also allowed to erect memorials to themselves in the sanctuary, although in the form of painted portraits hung in Hera's temple rather than statues. The champions' parents might even have commissioned victory odes. (The poet Corinna, a contemporary of Pindar's, may have written several; she is said to have beaten Pindar in a poetry competition in Delphi, prompting him to abuse her as "a Boeotian sow.") But beyond these shreds of information, the festival is a mystery. We do not know at what time of year the women's Games were held, or for how long they continued; some historians have speculated that they were actually simultaneous with the men's Olympics.

The Coed Gymnasium

WE CAN IMAGINE the frustration of some Greek women, since outside of Olympia they were allowed a more prominent role in the sporting culture. The teenage girls of Cyrene, for example, competed with the boys in footraces, and on the island of Chios they also wrestled. And the participation of women in Greek athletics appears to have increased in the Roman era, when women's events were added to most municipal festivals, and even infiltrated the sacred games of Corinth, Delphi, and Nemea. In a monument inscription from A.D. 45, a proud father boasts about his three daughters—named Tryphora, Hedla, and Dionysia—who won a string of footraces at Delphi and Corinth. But Olympia remained conservative to the end, maintaining its ban on female athletes and married women spectators. For twelve hundred years, the single loophole by which women could compete was, as we know, by entering the equestrian events as owners. (The feisty Spartan princess Cynisca had been the first to do so, and she set up a memorial to herself, crowing: "I place my effigy here / And proudly proclaim / That of all Greek women / I first bore the Olympic crown.") In the latter centuries of the Games, the restriction on married women spectators must have exasperated Roman women traveling in Greece, since they were allowed to sit with men back home in the arena of the Circus Maximus; at the gladiatorial fights in the Colosseum, female spectators were given a separate tier.

There was only one place in antiquity where girls received full physical education: Sparta. From its earliest days, this militaristic city in the central Peloponnesus wanted its women healthy. Along with their brothers, girls were taken from the family home at age seven and inducted into a grueling regime aimed at physical perfection. They were taught all the key Greek sports, including the javelin, discus, and wrestling, so that (one Greek author noted) "they were freed from all delicacy and effeminacy." They worked out at the gymnasium alongside boys, oiled down and naked, and wrestled with one another in municipal competitions. Spartan girls were even given some education in the arts and letters. They became as notorious around Greece for their muscular physiques as for their directness (the women of Sparta would exhort their husbands and sons before battles to return "with your shield or on it").

Their brazenness shocked the misogynistic Greeks. The "democratic" Athenians, for example, kept their girls cloistered away at home as securely as if they were captives of Islamic purdah, without even basic education; only radical thinkers like Plato would suggest that women might have an active role in society. Even when Spartan girls weren't running naked in the fields, Athenian moralists gasped, they wore short tunics without undergarments. They were nicknamed *phainomerides,* "thigh flashers," by the poet Ibycus in the sixth century B.C., and the scandalous epithet stuck. (The thigh was a euphemism for the female pudenda). They were reputed to be shamelessly promiscuous—after all, wasn't the most famous Spartan woman in literature the faithless runaway, Helen of Troy? As a character in a Euripides play rails to a Spartan of their unruly adolescent girls: "Why, they desert their homes and go out with young men with their thighs bared and their robes undone, and they hold races and wrestling contests with them! I would not stand for it! Is it any wonder that you Spartans do not raise chaste women?"

This hardly meant that Sparta was a proto-feminist paradise. The sole purpose of their training was to create physically fit mothers who would breed a superrace of powerful male soldiers. The purpose of their athletic training was, according to one observer, so that their progeny would take "a strong beginning in strong bodies." Women were given no alternatives by the "Controllers of the Women"—six shadowy officials whose task it was to ensure that the family production line was not interrupted by deviant females who might shirk their social duties. The nude exercises were contrived as a form of erotic advertisement to attract husbands, and any girl who tried to escape marriage was severely punished. It was all part of a ruthless eugenic system the Nazis would one day admire: When a Spartan baby was born, it was brought before a council—all male—and the physically inferior tossed down a ravine.

BUT BEFORE WE judge the Greeks too harshly, it should be remembered that even in the modern Olympics, women's equality has been a long time coming. The reviver of the Games, Baron Pierre de Coubertin, opposed having any women's events at all. They were not included in the 1896 Athens events; in 1900, women competed only in tennis; in 1904, tennis was dropped and replaced by archery. It was not until the 1928 Games at Amsterdam that women's track-and-field events appeared. Women's long-distance races were not permanently introduced until 1960 at Rome—and a women's marathon not until 1984 at Los Angeles.

XVI

Theater of Pain— the Contact Sports

He prayed to Zeus, "Give me victory or give me death!"
And here in Olympia he died, boxing in the Stadium,
At the age of 35. Farewell!

—MEMORIAL TO A BOXER KNOWN AS THE
"CAMEL OF ALEXANDRIA," FIRST CENTURY B.C.

"AND NOW COURAGE is needed," said the poet Statius; "valor here comes closest to that of battle and the sword." It would have been around noon on day four when it was announced in the Sacred Grove that the judges had taken their seats for the "combat" sports—wrestling, boxing, and the *pankration.* These were the signature events of the Greek athletic tradition, born from military training, practiced by every able-bodied male citizen in the *palaestra,* or wrestling school, and as formally stylized as any Eastern martial art. The crowds packing the Stadium meadow knew they were in for a grand human drama: The trio of contact sports were ferocious, vicious, and dangerous, regularly provoking injuries, even fatalities. Athletes were exempt from homicide charges, and every year there would be cremations after the festival. Wrestlers usually only ended up with cauliflower ears and broken noses, but *pankratiasts* could have their bones broken or be legally asphyxiated (the judges, says Philostratus, "approve of strangling"). And yet, the most lethal of the trio was held to be boxing, since athletes pummeled one another's heads for hours, with their knuckles wrapped in nothing but leather thongs. The god Apollo may have been the patron deity of pugilists, but mortal proponents rarely shared his divine good looks. Stories abound of champions emerging toothless and battered, their faces pounded to a raw pulp; epigrams told of an aristocratic Roman boxer who was denied his inheritance because none of his brothers could recognize him.

These life-and-death stakes added to the thrill. As Pindar said, "Deeds that involve no risk bring no honor either."

Descendants of Hercules

THE SIXTEEN WRESTLERS who paraded out of the entrance tunnel were hulking figures compared with the morning's run-ners—barrel-chested, ox-necked, and with muscles (one poet said) "the size of boulders." There were no weight divisions in Greek wrestling, so Olympic contestants tended to be heavy-weights all. In his training manual, the coach Philostratus men-tions that the wrestlers were given nicknames according to their different types of physiques, like "the bear," "the eagle," and "the lion" (the latter, for example, had strong arms but a weak back, daring in the attack but losing heart at any setback). Personal character, as dictated by the four bodily humors, was just as im-portant as strength for a champion. Those whose bodies were high in phlegm made good wrestlers, Philostratus said, but those who were choleric were too emotional, with the potential even for insanity. Philostratus, as ever, is also concerned with aes-thetics: A short neck looks bovine, he warns, while a straight back is beautiful, as is "a solid thigh turned outwards." "Narrow buttocks are weak," he adds, "fat ones slow, but well-formed but-tocks are an asset for everything." (Few may have lived up to the coach's high standards. An extraordinary mosaic from the Baths of Caracalla in Rome depicts a group of wrestlers in the second century A.D.—they are an unappealing bunch of bruisers, bulked up on their high-protein diets like force-fed pâté geese, looking lethargic, doltish, and pinheaded.)

At Olympia, the sixteen contestants had their hair cut short to escape the clutches of opponents; some wore leather skullcaps, clipped under the chin. Their bodies were oiled, but patted with colored powder to provide a good grip—the body palette ranged from yellow to orange, ochre, and brown—although some athletes secretly wiped an oily hand over a shoulder or thigh to skew an opponent's hold. Each wrestler drew a lot from a silver urn while muttering a prayer to Zeus, not looking at it until everyone had drawn; then the judges went around and paired off the eight opponents by the lot, alpha with alpha, beta with beta, and so on. If there was an odd number of contestants, one drew a bye—an enormous advantage, since he entered the second round fresh. The first pair then approached the flat, sanded wrestling ground in the Stadium.

The wrestlers moved into position, heads down, locking their arms together (as Homer says) "like gable rafters on a roof." The poet depicts Ajax versus Odysseus:

> *Their backs creaked under the strain*
> *Of their strong intertwined arms. Sweat*
> *Poured down their bodies, and bloody welts*
> *Rose up on their shoulders and ribs . . .*

The athletes' grunts and groans echoed around the arena as they feinted, parried, and shifted balance. This was what Greeks called "upright wrestling": holds had to be above the waist, although foot trips were allowed, and victory was achieved by throwing an opponent three times. A fall was declared whenever a contestant touched the ground with his hip, back, or shoulders.

It was the most gentlemanly of the three contact sports, with no punching, kicking, or gouging of "tender parts." Excited spectators yelled encouragement and laid bets; with each fall, clouds of dust rose and a thunderous roar went up. (Oddly, the modern Olympic sport called "Greco-Roman wrestling" has slightly different rules: Unlike ancient wrestling, it forbids foot trips.)

We know the favorite Greek wrestling moves from vase paintings: The Athenian hero Theseus, killer of the Minotaur in the Labyrinth of Crete, was credited with inventing wrestling, and is often depicted using classic holds on his enemies, while Hercules is shown employing the full repertoire of wrestling-school moves against sea monsters and lions. There was the familiar "flying mare," when a wrestler would take his opponent's arm and toss him over his shoulder, sending the victim crashing flat on his back. The dreaded "body hold" involved a wrestler gripping his opponent by the waist, hoisting him up, flipping the body in midair, then tossing him to the ground—most devastatingly, headfirst. (The ancient Greek expression "to hold him around the waist" meant having someone at your mercy.) Then there were the elaborate trips, where footwork and fast thinking could send a stronger opponent crashing down to the earth. The old-school wrestlers disdained these fancier moves. "Other wrestlers are mere stylists," crowed one memorial. "I win by sheer strength, as is only right and proper for a Spartan youth."

The rounds passed quickly, reducing the field from sixteen to eight, then four, until the two exhausted finalists faced off for the crown. On rare occasions at Olympia, a celebrity strongman would have so impressed the Greek wrestling community during the preliminary training period that nobody dared face him in the Games. On the morning of day four, he would find himself unopposed in the Stadium, and so proclaimed victor "without touching the dust." When this happened to the popular Milo of Croton, he approached the judges to accept the victory ribbons, but slipped and landed on his hip. Spectators joked that he shouldn't win because he had taken a fall.

A judge steps out of the way as a wrestler performs a throw known as the "flying mare." (From two damaged Greek drinking cups of the fifth century B.C.)

Milo was the only Greek wrestler ever to win five Olympic championships, in the late sixth century B.C.; he was finally defeated on his sixth attempt, at the age of forty. He served with distinction as a general in southern Italy, but eventually fell victim to his own vanity. Walking alone one day in the countryside, he saw a dried tree trunk split open with wedges, and to prove his strength he decided to break the trunk in two. Unfortunately, the wedges slipped out, Milo's hands were trapped in the tree, and wolves came and devoured the greatest Olympic champion in the night. Other Greek wrestling heroes had even more dubious IQ levels. An Olympian named Polydamas even tried to emulate the god Atlas by holding up the roof of a cave during an earthquake. His companions easily ran to safety, but Polydamus was killed when the cave collapsed. As Homer wisely said, those who live by their strength are doomed to perish by it.

Rumble in the Meadow

MEANWHILE, THE SIXTEEN boxers were putting on their gloves—a time-consuming process that required a trainer's full attention. The traditional versions were made with ten-foot leather thongs, softened with oil or animal fat and wrapped around the fist and wrist. These misleadingly named "soft gloves" were used to protect a boxer's knuckles rather than an opponent's face. Then, around 400 B.C., an even more formidable prototype came into fashion: called the "sharp glove," it had tougher leather thongs wrapped around a sheepskin cast that extended up the forearm, and bunched closely around the fist to create an effect like a modern knuckle-duster. These fearsome accessories were nicknamed *myrmekes,* "ants," for their sharp sting and their ability to slash the skin. The sheepskin on the forearm was used to wipe away sweat and blood in a bout. (Romans are credited with inventing an even more vicious glove, the *caestus,* which had metal weights and even spikes on the knuckles, but historians debate how often it was actually used.)

Again, boxers drew lots to select opponents, and the first contenders took their guard—vase paintings show them facing sideways, their left hand extended forward, right hand bent back and level with the shoulder, like freestyle swimmers in the middle of a stroke. A little psychological intimidation was not uncommon. The war cry of Epeius before his bout in *The Iliad* outdoes even Muhammad Ali: "Anybody fights me / I'll bust him wide open and crush his bones. Better have his next of kin standing by / To carry him out when I'm through." The opponents touched gloves together before the three judges, "breathing out mutual slaughter" (writes one poet); and then, says Homer, they went at each other:

> They stepped into the middle with hands held high
> And were all over each other with flurries
> Of hard punches, snapping jabs to the jaw,
> And the sweat was flying from their arms and legs.

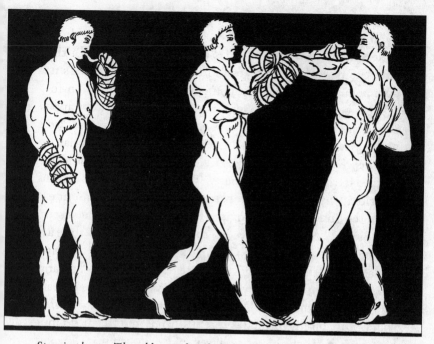

Sparring boxers. The athlete on the left *fastens the thongs of his glove with his teeth while awaiting his turn. (From an Athenian amphora, 336 B.C.)*

The Olympic rules were drawn up in 688 B.C., creating a scene quite different from modern boxing matches. The Greeks had no ring, so nobody was ever "pushed to the ropes"; boxers would range around the Stadium (although if they went too far astray, the judges would hold out rods at knee height to contain the fight). There were no rounds—the match kept going until one boxer was knocked senseless or admitted defeat by raising the middle finger of his right hand. But the main reason ancient boxing was so much more deadly than its modern equivalent is that the Greek rules specifically banned body blows: Punches were always aimed at the head. (The reason for this may have been the sport's military origins. The Spartans were said to have invented boxing to train their soldiers to fight without helmets, toughening their heads and teaching them to dodge blows.) Boxers could also use the sides of their hands as well as the knuckles to strike, and there was no restriction on mercilessly pummeling a boxer who was on the ground.

Most bouts actually began rather slowly. "The boxers didn't fall at once to angry blows," says Statius, "but stayed a while in mutual fear, and mingled caution with their rage." Only the inexperienced tried to force the pace. But soon enough, the fights reached dizzy heights of brutality. The poet Quintus Smyrnaeus describes "the streaks of sweat and blood [making] crimson bars down the flushed faces" of competitors, although good footwork, said Statius, could help evade "the thousand deaths that flit around the forehead." The Olympic champion Melancomas of Caria raised defensive tactics to an art: He was able to keep his guard up for a full two days at a time, forcing his opponents to give up from exhaustion. Almost alone among Greek boxers, he could boast on his memorial that his handsome face had never been scarred. At the opposite extreme, the masochistic Diogoras of Rhodes took pride in never dodging a blow, turning his features into a battered wasteland. But even he was outdone by Eurydamas of Cyrene, who had all his teeth knocked out in one Olympic bout—but rather than spit out his shattered enamels, Eurydamas swallowed them, to deny his opponent any satisfaction.

Greek spectators, as ever, went into paroxysms of enthusiasm during the bout. Many rushed down from their hillsides, gathering around the two swaying boxers, yelling, screaming, sparring alongside them, pushing so close they could almost touch their arms and taste the flying sweat. A great boxing match would go down in history, to be discussed by aficionados for centuries, and like today's fans, the Greek crowds loved to see strong, slow boxers pitted against lighter, faster opponents. These bouts were often re-created in literature: The poet Theocritus describes a brawl between one of Jason's Argonauts, Polydeukes, and a muscle-bound giant named Amykos. The giant "rushes in with all his might with wild blows, and exhausts both arms in the attacks with a fruitless gnashing of teeth," but Polydeukes sidesteps the attacks, then starts landing short, sharp jabs to the giant's face, pummeling him until he is almost blind, before finally hitting home with a devastating blow that "laid bare (the giant's) forehead to the bone."

At Olympia, the crowd particularly loved to see an underdog show some fight. "The spectators shriek out encouragement and bob and weave and punch together with the weaker contestant," says Philostratus. "And if he happens to land a lucky blow on the stronger boxer and actually mark the stronger man's face, they jump up and down in delirious excitement." But they were also notoriously fickle. In 212 B.C., an unknown Greek-Egyptian boxer named Aristonikos started out with the mob's support loudly behind him when he took on the famous Kleitomachos of Thebes. (Sports fans were "delighted that someone had dared, even for a moment, to stand up to the champion," say the chronicles.) But as the newcomer began landing solid punches, Kleitomachos grew sick of the partisan mob. During a breather, he turned angrily on the crowd, asking them why they were so keen on the weaker man. "Did they think he, Kleitomachos, was not following the rules? Or did they not grasp that he was fighting for the fame of Greece, and that Aristonokos was fighting for the fame of King Ptolemy? Did they really want to see an Egyptian win the crown at Olympia? Wouldn't they prefer a Theban be proclaimed the boxing victor?"

"When Kleitomachos had spoken in this way," reports Philostratus, "there was such a change in the crowd's feelings that it was their cheers rather than Kleitomachos' blows that finally beat Aristonokos."

SOME BOXING MATCHES ended abruptly, as did the bout that Homer describes in *The Iliad,* Epeius versus Euryalus:

> *As his opponent looked for an opening,*
> *Epeius moved in and got him with an uppercut,*
> *And Euryalus' legs were no longer under him . . .*
> > *His friends*
> *Dragged him through the crowd with feet trailing,*
> *Spitting out clots of blood, head hanging to one side.*

Other poets describe boxers falling "like slain oxen." Statius describes a fighter who knocks his opponent down, then keeps hitting as he tries to get to his feet. "Quick! Drag him off!" cry audience members. "He won't stop until he pounds the brain within the shattered skull!" Other bouts continued to the point of exhaustion. Boxers fell back by mutual agreement to regain their breath and have their faces sponged down, then lurched back to the fray. If a fight was going on too long, the judges separated the contestants and ordered them to take turns landing undefended blows—hardly a humanitarian solution. In one famous tiebreaker at Nemea, a certain Demoxenos of Syracuse jabbed out with his outstretched fingers, pierced the skin covering his opponent's rib cage, and pulled out his intestines. The judges denied Demoxenos victory, not for killing the other boxer but on the obscure technicality that he had actually struck four blows—one for each of his fingers.

No Holds Barred

IF WE CAN judge a Greek sport's popularity by the amount of cash offered to victors, the *pankration* was the top spectator sport in the ancient world; at the myriad prize games around the Mediterranean, it regularly attracted two to three times the award money offered for other events. It was a spectacular mix of wrestling and kickboxing, and because victory was achieved only by forcing an opponent to concede, inflicting maximum pain was the avowed goal. There was little the Olympic rules did not allow *pankratiasts:* armlocks and leg twists; punches to any part of the body; kicking, even to the groin. Strangulation was universally regarded as the most efficient means to achieve surrender. And yet, contrary to our perception of a brutal all-out brawl, the *pankration* had developed among the Greeks into the greatest test of skill, combining supreme strength with the balletlike style of kung fu.

Because of its obvious danger, the *pankration* was played out on a special soft-surface court: In the Olympic Stadium, teams of attendants chopped the earth with picks and applied water to create a sticky mud nicknamed "beeswax." The finalists drew their lots, and the first pair faced off across the mire.

According to accounts, the initial pace was frantic rather than calculated, as competitors lunged forward with furious energy, trying to land an early devastating kick or an agonizing armlock that would knock the other out of the match. In 364 B.C., an athlete named Sostratos of Sicyon used the tactic of breaking op-

A pankratiast raises the finger to admit defeat; at right, a trainer is making sure that the judge has seen. (From a Greek amphora, c. 520 B.C.)

ponents' fingers to force surrender. Nicknamed *Akrochersites,* "Mr. Digits," he won three Olympic victories in succession. (Although his attacks were quite legal, other athletes did not follow Sostratos's lead, and it appears audiences began to regard his tactic with disdain.) After crashing together, many *pankratiasts* ended up on their knees where, covered head to toe in mud, they would squirm, thrash, and grapple. Unlike standard wrestling, holds could be below the waist and, instead of counting falls, the contest continued until one athlete raised the finger and admitted defeat. An efficient road to victory was the ladder hold, where an athlete jumped on his opponent's back, wrapping his legs around the stomach; he could then lock his arms around the neck and block off the victim's breathing. Some agonizing footholds were used. They were invented by a short *pankratiast* from Cilicia, who was told by an oracle that he could win any match simply "by being trampled on." At first the Cilician was puzzled, but then realized that if he himself went beneath an opponent's feet, he could throw him and keep twisting his feet until he yielded.

There is no doubt of the extreme degree of viciousness involved. Vase paintings show *pankratiasts* with rivers of blood flowing from their noses and palm prints in blood across their backs; one contemporary describes them falling on one another "with the weight of a collapsing mine shaft." The brutality was further enhanced by the fact that it was considered a point of honor at Olympia to endure pain, resulting in some particularly gruesome injuries. Legs would be twisted from sockets, shoulders dislocated, ribs cracked and broken. Some *pankration* matches ended only at nightfall, in draws: When Tiberius Claudius Rufus from Smyrna held out until dark against an opponent who had drawn a bye in the previous round, the Elians passed a decree in his honor. And those athletes who chose death over defeat were always highly revered. Perhaps the most beloved *pankration* victor in the entire history of the Olympics was a man we have met before, named Arrhichion: In the final of

564 B.C., he was caught in a lethal ladder hold and was expiring from asphyxiation. Inspired by a shout from his trainer, Arrhichion managed to roll over and give his opponent's foot a savage twist. The opponent raised the finger of surrender just as Arrhichion died. Naturally, the judges awarded victory to the corpse. It was said that he went to the grave with the *pankration* dust still on him.

Like the Olympic runners, athletes in the combat sports loved to accrue bravura titles. In mythology, Hercules had won both the wrestling and *pankration* at Olympia, so anyone who repeated the feat was called "Successor of Hercules." Victors in all four of Greece's Sacred Games, at Delphi, Corinth, Nemea, and Olympia, were called *Periodonikes,* meaning "Circuit Champion," or *Paradoxos,* which translates, simply, as "Marvelous."

But as the day's happy victors went off to their brightly lit banquets, we can imagine another room at Olympia—one littered with the wounded.

XVII.

Bring on the Leeches...

Beware of doctors! They were the ones who killed me.
— Inscription on Roman gravestone, first century A.D.

ANCIENT GREEK MEDICINE was an amalgam of the rational and the mystical. Hippocrates, the Father of Western Medicine (c. 460–380 B.C.), famously introduced a scientific approach to the art of healing, but treatment for sports injuries remained inescapably riddled with superstition and philosophical fantasy. Ancient doctors aimed to balance the four "humors," or juices, within their patients' bodies—blood, phlegm, yellow bile, and black bile (a principle that remained the basis of Western medicine until the nineteenth century)—while medical advice from the gods, delivered to the sick via dreams, was paramount.

A resident physician was always listed on the roster of Olympic officials. At the Games, he would have been assisted by several *gymnotribai*—workers who attended Greek gymnasia, and therefore had practical knowledge of first aid. These pioneer paramedic teams must have been busiest on day one, after the equestrian events in the Hippodrome (the doctor Galen reports regular injuries among chariot drivers and jockeys to the chest, kidneys, and pelvis—although many broke their necks and were instantly killed). Day four was also busy, when wrestlers came in with their sprains, boxers with their battered faces, and *pankratiasts* with every possible injury. And it wasn't just the athletes who might need treatment. Apart from the risk from poorly aimed javelins and discuses, spectators faced a real danger of food poisoning, dysentery, sunstroke, and even attacks of malaria. As we know, the illustrious philosopher Thales of Miletus died of dehydration at Olympia; no doubt many lesser lights collapsed, their deliriums unrecorded by posterity.

In every Greek city and sanctuary, there was an *iatreia,* healing place. Archaeologists cannot confirm its location at Olympia, but the edifice referred to today as the "Greek Building," between the Stadium and Hippodrome, would have been the logical choice. Over the five days of the festival, it must have taken on the air of an army hospital—in fact, many first aid treatments for athletes were directly translated from the battlefield.

Greek doctors lacked anesthetics, although aspirin had been found in willow bark, useful as a mild painkiller and fever reducer, and opium had filtered into Greece in small quantities from the East. They also had little understanding of bacterial infections. But today we would recognize many of their practical procedures: Splints were devised for broken bones; stitches used for serious cuts; bandages, made from soft lamb's wool, applied to all wounds. Sprains were treated by "healer-masseurs"—the pioneer physiotherapists. In less orthodox practices, athletes with dislocated joints were hung upside down from ropes. Doctors could consult papyrus texts: The monographs of Hippocrates included helpful works such as *On Wounds to the Head,* while others listed remedies "useful around the wrestling field." Leeches were applied to minor injuries like sprained ankles, while more serious conditions called for purges, enemas, or tedious all-lentil diets.

A typical doctor's medicine chest overflowed with plant material, which had to be gathered under the correct phase of the moon by professional root cutters. Special herbs were added to staples like garlic, truffles, mushrooms, and the ashes of birds; an unguent made from dolphin liver was applied externally for skin ailments. Galen's second-century-A.D. work *The Composition of Medicines* includes one pharmaceutical he named, with early marketing flair, "Ointment for the Olympic Champion." Prescribed to ease muscular strains, the ingredients comprised raw egg mixed with aloe, saffron, cadmium, antimony, zinc oxide, frankincense, and myrrh to create a soothing (and sweet-smelling) paste.

Prognosis Divine

AS IN ALL aspects of ancient life, the Greek gods liked to dabble in medicine. Even the most rational pagan doctors recognized that crucial diagnoses for patients arrived in dreams, sent by Asclepius, the god of healing.

Unfortunately, it seems the deity had a sadistic streak. There are accounts of feverish patients, barely able to walk, being ordered by Asclepius in their dreams to jump into freezing-cold rivers, or to sail across a bay in the middle of a lightning storm, or to travel twenty miles to a temple of Apollo. Other patients were told to run a mile through snowbound forests, to fast for weeks, or to go without bathing for years. One serious problem was that the divine messages were often ambiguous. It was all very well if Socrates arrived in a dream and provided specific instructions, but what if one dreamed about being carried off by a giant bird, or dining with centaurs? The interpretation of such visions was a highly involved art, and in addition to its resident physician, Olympia had an official dream interpreter—not to mention dozens of itinerant experts attending the festival. Hypochondriacs could refer to the famous dream compendium of Artemidorus that listed common visions—for example, seeing a river overflow with blood—and their meanings. It's not surprising that Freud was fascinated by Artemidorus, praising him

as an early explorer of the unconscious. Oddly, Freud's own prud-
ish translation of the work left out the account of a man who
dreams he is having sex with his mother. According to Artemidorus, the nuances of this incest dream are crucial during an illness: depending on the sexual position, the dream could predict
recovery, death, or a simple falling-out with one's father.

NATURALLY, OLYMPIA'S MEDICAL staff had its limitations,
providing more of an ER-style, patch-them-up-ship-them-out
service. Injured athletes who required long-term care had to go
elsewhere for treatment—to one of the health sanitariums.

Contestants from Olympia would have to be transported by
wagon one hundred miles to Epidaurus, the most important
medical center in the pagan world. Although not as luxurious as
the great spas of Asia Minor, Epidaurus was most beloved by the
god Asclepius. An injured athlete would recuperate on the sanctuary floor for weeks or even months, bathing his feet in the sacred fountain, reclining on animal skins, and waiting for the
deity to grant him a vision. All around slithered harmless yellow
snakes—because they shed their skins, Greeks regarded them as
symbols of regeneration, the origin of their use as insignia for
modern doctors—while adopted dogs roamed among the patients licking open wounds, apparently with beneficial results.
The atmosphere was quiet and conducive to meditation. Like the
mountain sanitariums of Switzerland and Colorado in the late
nineteenth century, Epidaurus attracted wealthy patients who
spent their days writing epic verse as they were attended by a
host of physicians, phlebotomists, amulet makers, and palm
readers.

In contrast to this relaxed approach, one radical branch of
medicine combined a strict diet with hard-core exercise. It was
founded in the fifth century B.C. by Herodicus of Selymbria, who
had apparently cured his own mortal illness. Not all Greeks were

fans. "In his absurd melange of gymnastics and medicine," Plato notes caustically, "Herodicus found a way of torturing first himself and then the rest of the world, inventing a lingering death."

If an athlete did receive the healing god Asclepius in a dream, fees for service were the touchiest part of the relationship: Visitors had to leave a generous offering at Epidaurus or face the consequences. (One cheapskate who pretended he was penniless ended up with the scars on his face growing twice as deep as before.) Few took the risk. Dozens of bronze plaques have been excavated at the sanctuary attesting to the divinely inspired cures; they would be hung on the temple walls along with tiny models of the cured limbs and body parts, offerings from grateful patients.

XVIII

Last Rites

And then the strict judges, fulfilling the ancient
ordinances of Hercules, set the
gray ornament of olive upon the victor's hair.
—PINDAR, *Olympian Ode*

THE LAST DAY of the festival dawned on the wreckage of another long night of partying, with revelers curled up in corners like corpses and dogs picking over the putrefying garbage. Hungover wrestlers, boxers, and *pankratiasts* who rose to give thanks at the altar of Hercules were joined by another victor from the day before—winner of a peculiar ancient contest called *hoplitodromia,* or race-in-armor. The last sporting event of the Games, named after the Greek foot soldiers called hoplites, it was taken rather less seriously than regal contact sports. The contestants, who had not been required to go through the rigorous Olympic training, donned ceremonial bronze armor, then clunked up and down two laps of the Stadium. The race was famously clumsy, with runners banging into one another, dropping their shields, losing their helmets, and tripping. Whether or not the scene was regarded by Greeks as laughable, the race certainly inspired gently mocking references: In Aristophanes' comedy

The Birds, a character likens the Chorus figures, who are dressed up in feathered costumes, to the runners-in-armor.

Now, on day five, dignity would return in Olympia—in the form of prestigious award ceremonies.

In the Temple of Zeus, olive wreaths were laid out on an ivory and gold table. These crowns were almost mythological items: In a traditional ritual, they had been cut from Zeus's sacred tree by a young boy, both of whose parents were alive, using a golden sickle. (Spectators at Olympia could admire the tree itself, which had been planted by Hercules, protected by a fence on the west side of the Sacred Grove.) Until this moment, champions had been identified among the crowd by victory ribbons on their arms and the pine branches they carried. Now, bathed and groomed, they entered the sanctum sanctorum of Olympia, where they were announced before Zeus and then had the olive wreaths placed on their heads. Reemerging, they were carried on the shoulders of their friends around the grove as musicians played and flower petals rained down.

To the Greeks, this was as close to deification as any mortal could come—and the glory could compound over generations. In 448 B.C., according to chronicles, the boxer Diagoras of Rhodes, Olympic victor sixteen years earlier, saw his two sons both win wreaths for the *pankration* and boxing. As the young men hoisted their father on their shoulders and put each of their laurel wreaths on his head, a member of the crowd shouted out, "You might as well go up to heaven, Diagoras; there's nothing greater for you to achieve on earth." And with a happy smile, Diagoras died on the spot.

After the wreaths had been presented, the champions would be escorted to a private feast hosted by the judges. It was held in a venerable banquet hall in the Prytaneion, the administrative center of the Games, whose every wall oozed tradition: In one wing, the eternal flame was kept burning; in another lay the archives of the Olympic Games, dating back to 776 B.C.; and all over the walls were fantastic relics and memorabilia from famous

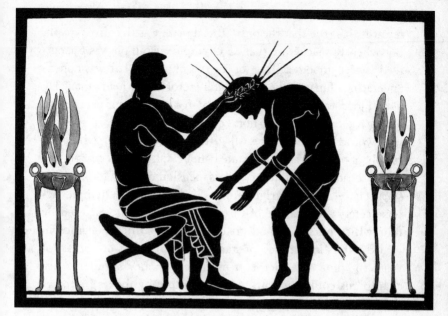

A champion accepts his wreath from a judge. Hanging from his arms are victory fillets, or ribbons. (From an Athenian amphora, c. 525 B.C.)

events, the discuses and javelins and gloves of heroes. The banquet was fit for demigods, and past victors were welcome to attend. One imagines the new victors sitting in such glorious company with distant eyes, thinking of their futures. Modesty was never an ancient virtue, and they eagerly gloated about their prospects.

The Road to Riches

AH, THE SWEET taste of immortality. An Olympic champion knew his name would be passed on from generation to generation, preserved in records throughout the known world, far better remembered than the names of kings or presidents today. There would be a victory statue to commission in Olympia—

perhaps an ego-boosting choral song. And there were material rewards. It's true that the only official prize was the olive wreath, but when Pindar wrote that an Olympic champion was guaranteed "sweet smooth sailing for the rest of his life," he was not exaggerating. Financially speaking, a victor was a made man. He would journey back to his home city in a triumphant parade, entering the gates in a four-horse chariot, where an adoring populace would shower him with gifts—cash rewards, a lifetime supply of oil, invitations to state banquets, front-row seats at the amphitheater, tax immunity, villas, pensions. In 416 B.C., the ecstatic city elders of Agrigentum in Sicily gave one Olympic victor a celebration parade of three hundred chariots, each led by four white horses. Proud cities engraved athletes' names in gilded letters in temples, or stamped their profiles on coins. For years to come, the victory would be a money spinner, since champions could rack up fortunes simply by making appearances at provincial sporting events. In the second century A.D., a small city in Asia Minor paid an Olympic boxer a staggering thirty thousand drachmas for a cameo bout (around one hundred times a Roman army soldier's annual pay); another offered fifty pounds of silver to a celebrity *pankratiast* just to show his face at their festival.

But why settle for mere money? Olympia was the perfect springboard for a career change, and a champion could easily become a judge, a priest, an ambassador. After his chariot win in 416 B.C., Alcibiades landed a plum military command in the invasion of Sicily. The great Theagenes of Thasos became a politician, styling himself as the "Son of Hercules"; in the Roman era, one Marcus Aurelius Asclepiades became a senator in Athens. Other victors were even hired as the emperor's personal trainer.

Just as a victor's fortunes soared, the prospects for the defeated were grim: They woke up on day five to a miserable horizon of failure. Good sportsmanship was thin on the ground in ancient Greece. There were no second prizes, no handshakes for a battle well fought. While the champions were being feted by the happy crowds, other, humiliated athletes slipped away from Olympia quietly, "skulking home to their mothers, traveling down back roads, hiding from their enemies, bitten by their calamity," wrote Pindar. Unlike the victors, their homecoming would be greeted by "no sweet laughter creating delight," but shame, embarrassment, and public mockery. As the *Oxford Classical Dictionary* laconically notes of these defeated athletes, "the incidence of failure-induced depression and mental illness was likely to be very high."

Perhaps the ultimate sore loser was the boxer Kleomedes, who, disqualified from his event in 492 B.C., "went out of his mind with grief." On his return to his home island of Astypalaea, he attacked a school building, pulling down a pillar and collapsing the roof on sixty boys inside. The angry townspeople came after Kleomedes with rocks, but he hid in a wooden box in the sanctuary of Athena. When it was smashed open, he had disappeared. In a surprise twist of events, the Astypalaeans consulted the oracle of Delphi, which told them that the deranged boxer was "no longer mortal." "From that day onwards," Pausanias observes, "the Astypalians worshipped Kleomedes as a hero."

The After-Party

THE CHAMPIONS MAY have clattered off in their gilded chariots, but for rank-and-file sports fans, as ever, getting home would not be so easy. Like the end of any mass spectator event today, anarchy descended on the site of Olympia as the hordes clogged the roads and haggled over the remaining transport. And yet, some willingly remained—the party animals who refused to let the revelry die. Apollonius of Tyana took up residence for forty days and forty nights, until he and his entourage ran out of funds to move on. His sidekicks were ashamed, but Apollonius simply strode into the Temple of Zeus and asked for one thousand drachmas, "if you do not think Zeus would be too annoyed." The priests generously replied that the only thing that would annoy the god would be if Apollonius did not take even more cash than he'd requested. One has the odd feeling they were glad to be rid of him.

The Cynic philosopher Peregrinus chose the postfestival period, with its captive audience, as the ideal time to publicly immolate himself in A.D. 165. He had announced his intention during the Games, saying that he was inspired by tales of the Indian Brahmans and their contempt for worldly values. The caustic Lucian mocked Peregrinus as a "publicity-mad fool"—"I wouldn't put it past him to jump out again half-cooked," another critic snickered—but still joined the curious crowd that got up at midnight and walked two miles to witness the moonlit suicide. As the old philosopher approached the pyre in his mendicant's rags, some observers were awestruck, others derisive of the grandstanding, still others drunkenly chanted, "Get on with it!" Looking pale, Peregrinus tossed incense into the flames, cried out, "Gods of my mother! Gods of my fire! Be gracious with me!" and leapt into the flames.

Lucian remained unimpressed—"I couldn't keep from guffawing," he says, nearly provoking a brawl with the philosopher's supporters—but Peregrinus had gained a place in Olympic history. Rumors soon circulated that the philosopher's ghost could be seen strolling the sanctuary in white robes and an ivy crown, smiling beatifically.

AS THE LAST stragglers left, laborers from Elis worked their way around the deserted site, antlike and determined, raking the Stadium, washing down the temples, using the wells they had dug before the Games as garbage pits. The rest of the debris, including the wooden frames of the vendors' booths and spectators' barracks, were burned.

The smoke from these great bonfires mingled with the last parched breaths of summer. We can imagine a stream of ash billowing across the ravines of Arcadia, dusting the brittle olive groves and rocky fields where goatherds contemplated their flocks, floating over the temples and the crags, the bone-white beaches and the abysses of blue, to the dark granite pillar of Mount Olympus in northern Greece, where the gods, in their palaces, were well pleased.

Champions and spectators were home in their distant hearths, but the clockwork of the seasons, of festivals and generations, continued on its course.

The organizers of Elis drew a deep breath—then began planning the next Games.

Time Line

THE STORY OF ancient Greece—and thus Western civilization—is intimately bound with the story of the Olympics. The Games went through many ups and down in their twelve-hundred-year history, but were never once canceled. By contrast, the modern Olympics have been suspended due to war three times since their revival—in 1916, 1940, and 1944.

Early Antiquity (c. 2500–776 B.C.)

c. 2500 B.C.—First settlement in Olympia region.

c. 1280 B.C.—Approximate date of Trojan War.

c. 1100 B.C.—Olympia becomes a cult site for Gaea, goddess of the earth, with agrarian and fertility festivals attended by local villagers.

c. 1000 B.C.—Worship of Zeus grows at Olympia, related to his oracle, which gives predictions on war; some casual athletic events take place at festivals.

c. 900–800 B.C.—Growth of the *polis,* or "city-state," in Greece, independent cities ruled by different forms of government—tyrants, oligarchies, and democracies.

The Archaic Age (776–479 B.C.)

776 B.C.—The first Olympic Games are proclaimed by King Iphitos of Elis, acting on the instructions of the Delphic oracle; the festival is offered to appease the gods and combat a plague that has been devastating Greece. The one and only event, a running race, is won by the Elian cook named Coroibos. (The date 776 B.C. was noted by the Greek chronicler Hippias of Elis; archaeologists suggest the Games may have begun slightly earlier.)

c. 750 B.C.—Homer composes *The Iliad* and *The Odyssey*.

570 B.C.—The city of Elis gains control over Olympian sanctuary (against the competing claims of the nearby Pisatans). Events at the Games are expanded.

508 B.C.—Athenian democracy established, a radical experiment in direct participation of male citizens in all government decisions and criminal trials. The result is a chaotic but highly creative civic life.

490 B.C.—First Persian invasion of Greece, ordered by King Darius. Against overwhelming odds, Athenians emerge victorious at the battle of Marathon. Olympia at this stage is a modest rural outpost with a single temple, dedicated to both Zeus and Hera, plus a few altars; athletic events are held in open fields and a rudimentary stadium.

480 B.C.—Second Persian invasion, led by Xerxes. The Olympic Games proceed despite the threat to Greece. Athens is sacked and the Acropolis burned—but the Persians are unexpectedly defeated by combined Greek forces in the naval battle of Salamis.

479 B.C.—Land battle of Plataea forces Persian withdrawal from Europe.

The Classical Age (479–323 B.C.)

476 B.C.—A celebration of Greek freedom combined with the Olympic Games consolidates the prestige of the festival. Building program begins at Olympia (including the erection

of the massive new Temple of Zeus, completed 459 B.C.; re-design of the Stadium; and creation of Phidias' statue of Zeus, completed c. 420 B.C.).

447 B.C.—Work begins on the Parthenon in Athens, a crowning achievement of the Golden Age under Pericles. The artistic ferment of Athens—in the arts, drama, science, and philosophy—leads to the Golden Age, funded by tributes from the city's growing naval empire.

431 B.C.—Commencement of Peloponnesian War, with Athens and Sparta as the main rivals. Greece begins to self-destruct.

404 B.C.—Surrender of Athens.

399 B.C.—Suicide of Socrates.

364 B.C.—Olympia becomes embroiled in Greek in-fighting; Elians and Arcadians fight a pitched battle in the sanctuary in the middle of the Olympic Games.

338 B.C.—Macedonia, led by King Philip, takes control of Greece after the battle of Chaeronea; end of the independence of city-states.

334 B.C.—Alexander the Great, Philip's son, begins his campaigns of conquest across the East, carrying Greek rule as far as the fringes of India.

323 B.C.—Death of Alexander in Babylon after a drunken feast.

Hellenistic Age (323–31 B.C.)

323 B.C.—Alexander's empire broken up into kingdoms ruled by Greek generals; Ptolemies rule Egypt as Greek-speaking pharaohs.

229 B.C.—First Roman incursion into Greece.

146 B.C.—Greek rebellion against Roman influence is crushingly defeated; the city of Corinth is leveled, all male citizens executed, and women and children sold as slaves.

144 B.C.—Olympic Games are held despite the new order.

80 B.C.—The Roman general Sulla pillages Olympia during civil wars fought on Greek soil; Greece is at a low ebb, as Roman armies repeatedly march across the country.

31 B.C.—Battle of Actium off Greece's west coast: Octavian, the future emperor Augustus, decisively defeats Mark Antony and Cleopatra, ending Rome's civil wars.

Roman Imperial Age

27 B.C.—Octavian proclaims himself *princeps*—"first citizen"—and takes the name Augustus. Pax Romana ushers in a new age of peace and prosperity. As Greek culture spreads more rapidly through the Roman Empire, athletics festivals are imported to Italy (as Horace famously said, "Conquered Greece took captive her barbarous conqueror").

A.D. 66—Visit of Emperor Nero, a devoted Hellenophile, to Greece; the emperor competes at the Olympic Games in A.D. 67, adding poetry to the roster of competitions.

c. A.D. 100—A second Golden Age of the Olympic Games emerges as emperors such as Hadrian lavish Olympia with gifts and buildings; in A.D. 150, the site even has its first efficient water system installed, ending centuries of discomfort for spectators.

The Gods Desert Olympia

A.D. 267—The Heruli, barbarians from southern Russia, invade the Peloponnesus of Greece; Elians put up a wall in the Sacred Grove to defend the sanctuary.

A.D. 312—Emperor Constantine makes Christianity the official religion of the Roman Empire; as paganism fades, the prestige of Olympia declines rapidly.

A.D. 365—The last Olympic victor on record is the Armenian prince Varazdates, who won the boxing in the 291st Olympiad.

A.D. 393—Last official Olympic Games (the 293rd). The victors' names are lost.

A.D. 394—The emperor Theodosius I bans all pagan festivals. The Olympics are officially disbanded—although archaeologists now suggest that they kept going in some form, perhaps in Christian guise. Phidias' great statue of Zeus is packed up and transported to Constantinople for display in the emperor's palace.

A.D. 426—Temple of Zeus burned on orders of Theodosius II. Christian fanatics destroy the rest of the sanctuary.

A.D. 475—Palace fire in Constantinople destroys the statue of Zeus.

A.D. 522—The first of several devastating earthquakes hits Olympia. In coming centuries, the rivers Alpheus and Cladeus regularly flood, burying Olympia under fifteen to twenty feet of yellow silt.

The Olympic Program

THE ORIGINAL FORMAT of the ancient Olympics was such a success that it hardly changed after its main contours were established around 470 B.C. There were a few ill-fated experiments, but by and large the schedule remained consistent, a beacon of Greek tradition in a world transformed by conquests, plagues, exotic religions, and grasping empires. Historians still argue about the details, but a consensus has emerged on the basic schedule of the five-day program:

Day One

A.M.
- Opening ceremonies: Swearing-in of athletes, trainers, and Olympic judges before a statue of Zeus wielding a thunderbolt.
- Contests for heralds and trumpeters in the Echo Colonnade.
- Athletes make their private sacrifices to the gods at one of the site's altars and consult oracles.

P.M.
- Free time for art lovers to explore Sacred Grove of Zeus, one of Greece's most spectacular collections of statuary and paintings.
- Literary events: Poets recite their works, philosophers expound, historians present new work.
- Less edifying pursuits available at the carnival-style festival fringe.

Day Two

A.M.

- Equestrian events: Chariot and horse races in the Hippodrome. The popular four-horse chariot race, or *tethrippon,* opens the celebration, followed by bareback races. In 408 B.C., a two-horse chariot race is added, followed in later years by a four-colt chariot race (384 B.C.), a two-colt chariot race (268 B.C.), and bareback races for colts (256 B.C.).

P.M.

- Pentathlon in the Stadium—a grueling event for all-rounders that combines discus, javelin, long-jumping, running, and wrestling.

Late

- Funeral ceremony for the hero Pelops at his burial mound in the Sacred Grove.
- Celebrations: Victory parades, choral hymns, banquets for champions.

Day Three

A.M.

- The Games' central religious ritual, coinciding with the full moon: an official procession to the Great Altar of Zeus, followed by sacrifice of one hundred oxen.

P.M.

- Boys' events (wrestling, running, boxing; after 200 B.C., boys' *pankration*).

Late

- Public banquet of sacrificed meat.

Day Four

A.M.

- Running races: 200, 400, and 3,600 meters.

P.M.
- Contact sports: Wrestling, boxing, and the *pankration.*

Late
- Race-in-armor.

Day Five

- Closing ceremonies: Wreaths are presented; victory processions; champions showered with leaves. Prestigious dinner for champions and officials, followed by general celebrations.

Sources

ALTHOUGH THIS IS meant to be a lively, entertaining account, I have made every effort to ensure that my reconstruction of the ancient Olympics is historically accurate.

For original ancient texts—Pindar's odes, Philostratus' *Life of Apollonius of Tyana,* the works of Aeschylus, Plato, Xenophon, Dio the Golden-Tongued, Herodotus et al.—I have generally referred to the standard Loeb texts published by Harvard University Press.

For Homer's *Iliad* and *Odyssey,* I have used Stanley Lombardo's translations, released by Hackett Publishing Co. (I personally regard these as the finest and most readable versions in modern English—each of Lombardo's lines captures the directness of Homer's language and crackles with vitality.) For Pausanias' *Description of Greece,* I use most often Sir James Frazer's excellent text published in six volumes in the Victorian era (reprinted by Biblo and Tannen, 1965), as well as occasionally referring to Peter Levi's more recent Penguin edition (1971). Lucian's caustic satire *Peregrinus* is best translated by Lionel Casson; for his *Anacharsis,* I use the Loeb text and sections by Stephen G. Miller. For Philostratus' work on gymnastics, I generally adapt an archaic edition by Thomas Woody. Many ancient inscriptions and fragments are referred to from Rachel Robinson's 1955 work, *Sources for the History of Greek Athletics,* and the indispensable, more up-to-date volume edited by

Stephen G. Miller, *Arete: Greek Sports from Ancient Sources;* Miller's creative insights on the documents often brought them to unexpected life.

As with any work of historical synthesis, I owe a great debt to dozens, if not hundreds, of other historians. Any re-creation of specific ancient sports builds on the pioneering work of Norman Gardiner; his *Athletics of the Ancient World* (1930) is the basis for all subsequent studies on the subject. My chapter on classical-era Greek travel could not have been written without Lionel Casson's seminal research in the field, especially his volume *Travel in the Ancient World.* I owe an even greater debt to James Davidson for his brilliant book *Courtesans and Fishcakes: The Consuming Passions of Classical Athens,* which guided me through the more licentious side of Greek festivals (especially drinking habits, banquet behavior, homosexuality, and prostitution). I would also like to single out Thomas F. Scanlon's work on women's athletics in ancient Greece, and David C. Young's writings on the myth of amateurism in the ancient Olympic Games.

A partial list of my secondary sources includes:

Birge, Darice E., Lynn H. Kryanak, and Stephen G. Miller, *Excavations at Nemea.* University of California Press, two volumes, 1999 and 2001.

Casson, Lionel, *Travel in the Ancient World.* Johns Hopkins University Press, 1994.

Davidson, James, *Courtesans and Fishcakes: The Consuming Passions of Classical Athens.* St. Martin's Press, 1997.

Finley, M. I., and H. W. Pleket, *The Olympic Games: The First Thousand Years.* Chatto and Windus, 1976.

Gardner, Norman E., *Athletics of the Ancient World.* Ares, 1930.

Golden, Mark, *Sport and Society in Ancient Greece.* Cambridge University Press, 1998.

Golden, Mark, *Sport in the Ancient World from A to Z.* London: Routledge, 2004.

Lee, Hugh M., *Nikephoros Beihefti: The Program and Schedule of the Ancient Olympic Games.* Weidmann, 2002.

Mandel, Richard D., *The Nazi Olympics.* New York, 1971.

Miller, Stephen G. (ed.), *Arete: Greek Sports from Ancient Sources.* University of California Press, 1991.

Raschke, W. J. (ed.), *The Archaeology of the Olympics: The Olympics and Other Festivals in Antiquity.* University of Wisconsin Press, 1988.

Robinson, Rachel Sargent (ed.), *Sources for the History of Greek Athletics in English Translation.* Cincinnati, 1955.

Romano, David Gilman, *Athletics and Mathematics in Archaic Corinth: The Origins of the Greek Stadion.* Philadelphia: American Philosophical Society, 1993.

Scanlon, Thomas, *Eros and Greek Athletics.* Oxford University Press, 2002.

Sinn, Ulrich, *Olympia: Cult, Sport, and Ancient Festival.* Princeton: Markus Weiner, 2000.

Swaddling, Judith, *The Ancient Olympic Games.* University of Texas Press, 1999.

Young, David C., *The Olympic Myth of Greek Amateur Athletics.* Chicago: Ares, 1985.

Index

Illustrations are listed in *italic* type.

ABOUT THE TYPE

This book was set in Garamond No. 3, a variation of the classic Garamond typeface originally designed by the Parisian type cutter Claude Garamond (1480–1561).

Claude Garamond's distinguished romans and italics first appeared in *Opera Ciceronis* in 1543–44. The Garamond types are clear, open, and elegant.